NOT OUT!

THE INCREDIBLE STORY OF THE
INDIAN PREMIER LEAGUE

DESH GAURAV SEKHRI

PENGUIN

VIKING

VIKING

Viking is an imprint of the Penguin Random House group of companies
whose addresses can be found at global.penguinrandomhouse.com

Published by Penguin Random House India Pvt. Ltd
4th Floor, Capital Tower 1, MG Road,
Gurugram 122 002, Haryana, India

Penguin
Random House
India

First published in Viking by Penguin Books India 2016

The views and opinions expressed in this book are the author's own and the facts
are as reported by him which have been verified to the extent possible, and the
publishers are not in any way liable for the same.

Please note that no part of this book may be used or reproduced in any manner
for the purpose of training artificial intelligence technologies or systems.

ISBN 9780670088737

Typeset in Sabon by Manipal Digital Systems, Manipal
Printed at Replika Press Pvt. Ltd, India

www.penguin.co.in

This is a legitimate digitally printed version of the book and therefore might not
have certain extra finishing on the cover.

To the memory of my father, Desh Deepak, whom we lost to cancer recently. He was an exemplary person and will be missed as a father, husband, father-in-law, brother, friend and grandfather. Dad, you lived a blessed life, and enriched ours by your presence.

Contents

Acknowledgements

Writing a book is a journey, and being a published author is a dream I have had for as long as I can remember. It hasn't been the easiest journey, but it has been made far more memorable because of the individuals who have helped and supported me as I learnt and developed. I learnt about how brevity is the soul of wit, and how I best expressed myself and my emotions through the written word. There are many whom I would like to thank for being there through this journey and for their support, and some to whom I am indebted. These are the people and institutions who helped me channel my ideas and opinions on topics of sport, and the most relevant topic since I have been involved with Indian sports is, of course, the Indian Premier League (IPL). I don't mean this to be a book dwelling on controversies and negatives—far from it. The IPL is in a unique position to achieve the impossible and consolidate its first-mover advantage like no other sports league in the history of sports globally. It is my fervent hope that the IPL turns towards solidity rather than scandal, and transparency rather than opaqueness. It isn't that difficult to achieve, and all of us would be the better for it.

Let me now express my gratitude. First of all, I would like to thank Penguin Random House for giving me the opportunity to put my scattered thoughts and abstract ideas to virtual paper. In particular, I must thank Premanka Goswami, who has brainstormed with me, guided me through the process, and essentially made this possible. During this experience, I sought out the advice and guidance of Nandita Aggarwal who was, and is, an invaluable mentor in the art of publishing. I thank her for tolerating me for over five years and indulging my many hare-brained ideas and literary aspirations.

Writing a book and having it published would have been impossible without the opportunities afforded to me by my mentors and friends in the media. I began writing on topics embracing the vagaries of sports law, the business of sports and other such obscure areas over seven years ago, and I still cannot believe that there was anyone willing to take a punt on me by publishing what were at best unsubstantiated and unorthodox ideas. I began writing for the Express Group, and to the entire editorial team I am forever indebted, as they allowed me to not only share my views but also to explore and develop new skills as a writer. I must explicitly express my gratitude to Saubhik Chakraborty, Raj Kamal Jha, Unni Rajan Shankar, Mini Kapoor and Mihir S. Sharma. And I am indebted, of course, to Shekhar Gupta, the group editor-in-chief at the time, and whose columns have been a constant source of inspiration for me.

I would like to thank Indi Hazra who has helped me hone my critiquing skills, and with whose encouragement I have become a columnist with expressive viewpoints on many of the topics that I have covered in this book. I must also mention my association with Gaurav Kalra and our interactions on cricket and the IPL. For his support and the opportunities he has given me to air my views, many thanks.

I'm not sure I would have ever taken myself seriously if Jyoti Sagar hadn't had the vision to encourage and enlist me for the purpose of building a sports law practice—something unheard of in 2009. Always supportive and frequently galled by my limited skills, Jyoti has been a visionary who gave me the platform at J. Sagar Associates, and for that I continue to be grateful. In the same vein, I want to thank my close friend, chief mentor and boss, Venkatesh Raman Prasad. Venky is a rare combination of brilliance, compassion and loyalty. He has been the sole reason for my having been able to stay the course for seven years in a nascent hyper-specialization, and I am proud to have him as a close friend, and lucky to have his support and advice in all facets. I must also thank the fearless Rahul Mehra, my close friend and colleague. He is without doubt the face of sports activism in India, and without his untiring effort, the evolution of Indian sports would be but a pipe dream. I am privileged to work closely with him and see the changes manifest. Also, I would like to thank Mr Vinod Rai for his support.

And now I get to those who mean the world to me, through blood or marriage. During the course of writing this book, I lost my father, and consequently am the only male member of a family filled with strong women—my mother, my sister, my wife and my infant daughter. I would like to thank my parents for their support and for allowing me to grow by experiences rather than by the text of books and cultural norms. I would like to thank my sister for being the foil during my disagreements with my parents (and there were many of them), and for being the third parent to an extremely spoilt child. At thirty-seven, I am still a petulant teenager, so it couldn't have been easy for any of them when I was growing up.

And lastly, this brings me to the person whom I am the most indebted—for making the active choice of choosing to be with me as my wife, to balance me, to stabilize me, to support me, to listen to me, to advise me, to tolerate me, to indulge me, and to weather me. I don't emote well in speech, so let me take this chance to thank you for being with me, for fighting for me, and perhaps even for fighting with me. Thanks, Madhavi, for being my support.

The Great Indian Roadshow:
The IPL Today

The Indian Premier League (IPL) is India's best known sports commodity. Some might call it infamous. In fact, former Delhi police commissioner Neeraj Kumar claims that three banned players of Rajasthan Royals— S. Sreesanth, Ankit Chavan and Ajit Chandila—arrested in the 2013 spot-fixing case were linked to Dawood Ibrahim via syndicates and bookies.[1] However, the IPL has transcended sports or even current affairs and it is embedded in the Indian social system, a replication of our culture—one that embodies all that we as Indians either hold dear or choose to shun. Today it has both evolved and regressed in a myriad of ways, almost unrecognizable from what was expected of it in 2007 when it stormed the collective Indian psyche. By the time IPL's ninth season comes around in 2016, much should have changed about it, but probably may not have.

The IPL has taken all of Indian society, thrown it into a blender, shaken it with some olives, and served it as a heady cocktail of intrigue, sport, games, controversy and general entertainment. If one looks at the who's who of Indian culture and society, be it from Bollywood, corporate India or the political diaspora, the IPL has been inclusive despite being exclusive. This has had its pros as well as its cons. By mixing different flavours of society, the IPL has made cricket even more entertaining than a typical Bollywood blockbuster, and its general entertainment appeal has been unparalleled. But with all the success, the IPL has had more controversy than its fair share, in a relatively short span of eight years. It has been an equal opportunity publicity juggernaut and scandal allocator. Sold to investors, sponsors and the general public as the total package, the IPL did initially meet the lofty expectations it set for itself. However, the accompanying churn in the administration, governance and on-field play made it a pariah in the eyes of many. Put simply, the IPL is an entity that is fashionable to dislike, but at the same time, is a regrettable necessity for Indian society. It's a necessity because it embraces so much of Indian culture that it is now synonymous with it. It's a regrettable necessity because it has been stature-blind in its ability to jilt careers, cause scandal and disrupt careers. Even its promoter, Lalit Modi, has seen some of the highest highs, and the deepest valleys in large part due to his association with the IPL. It is stature-blind because it has impacted the reputation of rising star politicians, put its stakeholders' personal matters into the public domain, killed the professional careers of talented cricketers, and brought scrutiny to the affairs of its administrators and investors alike. It has its supporters and its detractors, but on one point you can be sure that they all agree—the IPL is larger than life, and twice as loud. It is too popular to just be a fad, and has too many legitimate corporates investing in it to simply be labelled a racket.

So given the immense footprint of the IPL, the only obstacle in its way was itself, and as frequently happens, it has managed to trip itself up numerous times in the last few years, to the extent that it is now the focal point of a Supreme Court–appointed committee. Some of its franchises have been suspended, a few terminated, and its erstwhile administrator (Lalit Modi) and some of its team owners (including the Kolkata Knight Riders— KKR) have kept the Enforcement Directorate (ED) quite busy scrutinizing its activities. There is a perceived credibility gap with regard to this league; its flamboyant image and its creation of a parallel universe where money solves everything, and bigger is always greater, have put many people off. Not that its ratings or overall popularity has been shaken, but the IPL remains as much of interest for its off-field offerings as it does for the on-field sport. I'm not sure that's the best starting or selling point for a professional sports league, but with so many different avenues of revenue available to the league, it's unsurprising that the changes until recently have been few and mostly symptom-based solutions to manage the problems, not prevent or control them. Not everyone has found unqualified success within the IPL, and quite a few of its erstwhile sponsors and investors are no longer affiliated with it, for reasons that may or may not be the fault of the Board of Control for Cricket in India (BCCI) or the IPL. For now, let's look at the IPL in its present shape, and how it got to this point.

In 2015, the IPL was at the centre of numerous litigations, and more importantly, of judicial intervention by no less an authority than the Supreme Court of India. The powers that be of the BCCI have been admonished and even warned by the court which has appointed two committees to look into the affairs of the IPL and the cricket board itself—the Justice Mukul Mudgal Committee in 2013 and then the Justice R.M. Lodha Committee in 2015. Little however has changed in the several years that the IPL has held centre stage. In many ways, the IPL is still a nascent league—after all, eight years in the life of a professional sport entity isn't a lot. What has changed for the BCCI and therefore the IPL in recent years is that cricket in India has lost its aura of invincibility—and credibility to a large extent—despite its commercial might and overall popularity with the majority of India's populace. Cricket is the only sport in the world where the nucleus lies in India, and with the clout of almost a billion people supporting every ball bowled, boundary hit, or catch made, the power of Indian cricket is inarguable, unmistakable and non-negotiable. The IPL was meant to showcase the BCCI's overall dominance and project India as the centre of the world in cricket philosophy.

By now, the IPL should have had and exploited the massive first-mover advantage. It should have consolidated and optimized the revenue verticals that a tournament of this magnitude enjoys. The BCCI should have extended the reach of the IPL by adopting a top-down model where year-round visibility and the development of infrastructure, talent and commercial activity in T20 cricket should have been the norm. It should have accepted in 2008 itself that the only way forward for a global cricket property such as the IPL would be through emulating and initiating best industry practices of established professional sports leagues from which it had copied the glint- and glamour-driven attributes. It should have striven to ensure that the IPL was insulated from questionable practices/ownership of teams; and that its participants were properly oriented and educated on basic aspects of ethics, integrity and business dealings. Above all, the BCCI should have ensured that the IPL was operated as a professionally run organization with an accountable profit-making directive, independent in every way from the overarching interference of itself and its officials.

The tipping points

So much has gone wrong with the IPL over time that it is easy to forget how important a role it has played in Indian sports, and how beneficial it actually could have been for Indian society as a whole. Much has, of course, gone wrong due to the flawed priorities of the individuals who oversee the entire league. But more than anything else, there has been a consistently inconsistent manner of governance that is so clearly insufficient that most of what the IPL could have achieved has been lost due to gross negligence and misconduct. To blame this governance fallout on one person or regime is pointless and incorrect because none of the BCCI regimes have yet done much to rectify what so clearly has gone wrong.

There isn't any single reason that has led to the erosion of reputation and goodwill that the league could have commanded, but there are many reasons that have led to this situation. In a nutshell, what the BCCI did was somehow ignore best practices owing to a false sense of comfort that it was exempt from any rules and regulations that governed all other entities in India. It did or let others do things that shouldn't have been allowed or done, simply because, as the all-powerful governing body for cricket, it could. In doing so, it forgot about all semblances of accountability, transparency, integrity and good business sense, sacrificing viability for show-stopping entertainment. The IPL has tolerated sleaze, veiled and opaque ownership and investment, questionable authenticity of the matches itself, and rampant conflict of interest, all to remain entertaining and topical. Each regime, and each successive BCCI official at least until recently, has fallen prey to the glitz and the glamour of the IPL. And in doing so, it has triggered a culture of shock journalism, with the IPL's off-field activities often the showstoppers on prime-time television.

If one has to pinpoint the factors that have led to this fall from grace for the IPL and its creators, two incidents come to mind. These were the two incidents which made pariahs of two of the league's most vocal supporters within the BCCI, and are discussed in detail in Chapters 2 and 3. The Kochi franchise controversy of 2011 and the spot-fixing scandal of 2013 cost Lalit Modi and N. Srinivasan their respective positions of power in the BCCI–IPL. Could they have been prevented? Absolutely. Did either of the then omnipotent leaders feel they could have been toppled at any juncture? Certainly not. And because of these two incidents the entire basis of the IPL metamorphosed.

In 2015, the IPL was in strife. The root of the problem lay in the structure of the IPL itself, and everything else arose from it. For some unbeknownst reason, the IPL is structured as a subcommittee of the BCCI. The board therefore has influence over, and responsibility for, every aspect of the IPL's activities. It has hired professionals to oversee and market the league, but the basic business and governance principles, or the lack of them, have caused the IPL's foundation to be weak. Now it not only has to face multiple litigations, but the court is also actively involved, both directly and indirectly, in deciding the future course for the first official sports league of India.

In 2011, the Kochi fiasco stalled the league's growth, followed by the Pune franchise withdrawing in 2013. The year 2013 was when the IPL's reputation took a beating, primarily due to the spot-fixing scandal. The year 2016 may go down in history as the year when the Justice Lodha Committee in its recommendations transformed cricket administration and the governing of the IPL as we had known it thus far. I will address the recommendations in detail, through various sections. All said and done, aside from the judiciary's recent involvement, cricket in India has resembled an indigenized *Game of Thrones* where little has changed without external intervention. And the IPL is the loudest example of much that has gone wrong in Indian sport and Indian society. It has also been a rainmaker of sorts, bringing stashes of money to sport, and marrying every facet of Indian culture to each other while ensuring that cricket remains India's favourite pastime. In no other society in the world has so much depended on a single sporting event. It was this thirst for overarching sizzle, glitz, fame and power that has led to the partial decline of the IPL. Today it is very different from how it all began, and from when it peaked in 2010.

Modi's role and absentee ownership

It's best to begin by summarizing, in reverse chronology, the most relevant challenges that the BCCI faces today on account of the IPL. In September 2015, the *Indian Express* released leaked emails hinting at Modi's ownership in three franchises, including the Kings XI Punjab (KXIP).[2] The origins of this email pertained to an upcoming transaction involving the selling of the KXIP to an investor. As per the mail, it appears as if Modi is one of the owners of the franchise; he's copied on emails and is found to be taking an active role in furthering the KXIP's sale. Many were not surprised, as since the inception of the IPL it had been strongly rumoured that Modi had an ownership stake in more than a few franchises.[3] His connection with cricket in Rajasthan had always been known, and many felt that he was a faceless owner of the Rajasthan Royals (RR), whose official owners were the Emerging Media Group. His brother-in-law Suresh Chellaram owns/owned a significant stake in the franchise, and Modi's proximity to the Rajasthan Cricket Association (RCA) is well documented. His stepson-in-law, Gaurav Burman, is associated through his family with the ownership of the KXIP franchise. And his close friend, Jay Mehta, is a stakeholder in the Kolkata Knight Riders.[4] These are the three franchises that Modi was most close to.

A fourth association was rumoured to be on the cards when in 2010 Modi railed against the Kochi franchise and its owners, the Rendezvous Sports Group. It was alleged that Modi was dead against the Kochi franchise joining the IPL because he was involved in getting a franchise for Ahmedabad, to be owned by the Adani Group.[5] He was also at the time accused of favouring Videocon's bid, and the proof of this was said to be the two contentious clauses added by Modi to the bid documentation. One clause made the minimum net worth requirement for potential bidders a whopping US$1 billion, and the other clause required a bank guarantee of over INR 450 crore. Modi agreed that he had added the clauses, but said his rationale was to ensure that viable bidders entered the fray, given that the positive cash flow for franchises would begin only by the eighth season.[6] The tender was eventually scrapped after only two bids were received. The Kochi franchise debacle turned out to be a fatal one for its promoters and for Modi. Apparently, in his anger at having been bypassed during the franchise auction, Modi made it a point to take to social media to disclose the ownership pattern of the Kochi franchise's consortium. Not only was this alleged to be a breach of the confidentiality provisions of the franchise arrangement, it was an embarrassing revelation for both the consortium and for the BCCI.[7] Modi's claim was that Cabinet Minister Shashi Tharoor was involved in facilitating the transaction because he had an ulterior motive.[8] Tharoor at the time was said to be involved with one of the equity holders, Sunanda Pushkar, who had a sweat equity stake of approximately 4.75 per cent, according to one of Modi's many tweets on this subject. Modi's contention was that Pushkar's sweat equity component was actually veiling the actual ownership which Modi felt was Tharoor's.[9] The incident got escalated, and eventually, Tharoor was forced to resign from the Cabinet, and shortly after that Modi was suspended from the IPL and the BCCI for financial irregularities and bringing disrepute to the board.[10] Modi's suspension was later elevated to a life ban. The ban continued and Modi is also unable to return to India as the ED has initiated a probe which could eventually lead to imprisonment for him if he is found guilty. The Kochi franchise, which struggled to fix its ownership pattern to be in conformity with the IPL's requirement, was star-crossed. After a mediocre season in the IPL, it was unable to make its franchise fee payments, and in just its second year, it was terminated by the BCCI. There has been a reprieve for it in recent months, but more on that later.

Meanwhile, adding to the belief that Modi was involved in some capacity with some of the franchises, in late 2010, the BCCI–IPL decided to take matters into their own hands in the absence of Modi at the helm.[11] Citing multiple irregularities, the BCCI terminated the two franchises most closely associated with Modi—the KXIP and the RR. The matter went to court and the termination was overturned, thereby allowing both franchises to participate in the subsequent seasons of the IPL. What this appears to imply is that the faction opposing Modi either believed or suspected that the nexus between Modi and the two franchises was a strong one, although an official communication or statement by the board was not released.[12]

The Kochi fiasco provided Modi's detractors in the BCCI with a golden opportunity to rusticate him. For a man who was enterprising and in many ways fearless in the face of adversity, history may not view him in a favourable light, and he is likely to get a bad rap. But in all honesty, many of the harder-hitting rumours have not been conclusively proven until now. Even the judiciary and the court-appointed committees appear to have taken a forward-thinking approach when it comes to the IPL, and the focus now appears to be on reforming and reining in the truant nature of the board and the IPL rather than exorcising past ills. That's not to say if any irrefutable evidence of unethical behaviour arises against any of the IPL's protagonists, the courts and the committees will not act; but, using the Justice Lodha Committee as a reliable precedent, the interest of the game is paramount, and the future of cricket and the IPL must be secured. Modi would perhaps have played a part in introducing and perpetuating the culture which led to conflicts of interest and other governance lapses, but he surely wasn't the only one, and this book isn't about passing judgement or propagating a witch-hunt of errant participants in the game of IPL.[13] As for commercializing and monetizing Indian cricket and the IPL, Modi ought to get the credit for initiating and expanding it. He, of course, couldn't finish what he started. Modi's connection to the three franchises and the conspiracy theories that have been floated which apparently substantiate his involvement in the three franchises and the proposed franchise for Ahmedabad will be looked at closely in Chapter 3.

The spot-fixing scandal

In 2013, the IPL was faced with its biggest challenge, one that continues to threaten its existence. The spot-fixing scandal of 2013 will forever be the watershed moment for cricket in India, when arguably the biggest and most impactful controversy to hit Indian sports reared its ugly head. But it was the various governance and transparency lapses leading up to 2013 that had actually led to a tipping point. Hindsight will always be 6/6, but little was done to right the course, and it was clear that the IPL was getting careless and callous. The IPL has, in many ways, made more enemies for the BCCI than friends, and the resentment at the lopsided enrichment that has ensued for the board only makes the future more difficult.

The spot-fixing scandal erupted in May 2013 during IPL VI, after the Delhi Police concluded that three members of the RR—Ajit Chandila, Ankit Chavan and S. Sreesanth—had been in touch with bookies and received money to fix matches in the IPL. The three were arrested, as were numerous bookies, and the web of spot-fixing and illegal gambling/betting on the outcome of IPL matches was cast. It was just the beginning. As the nexus between bookies, players and player agents was analysed, the investigation expanded beyond the obvious parties, and extended to team owners and officials. It was that critical connection that began the downfall in the BCCI of Modi's nemesis and successor, Srinivasan. Organized crime syndicates, socialite conduits and, most importantly, team owners of two of the franchises—the RR and the Chennai Super Kings (CSK)—were brought under the purview of the interrogation, and the results were devastating. Gurunath Meiyappan, the son-in- law of Srinivasan and widely considered to be the owner or team principal of the CSK, was alleged to have shared sensitive information, bet on matches, and even attempted to influence matches. Srinivasan, the president of the BCCI, quickly distanced himself from his son-in-law's activities, and dismissed all allegations that Meiyappan was a team official or team principal of the CSK. Meiyappan was described as a 'cricket enthusiast' and it was stated that he held no real official role with the CSK. This was, of course, hardly believable, but it was a stance that Srinivasan maintained until well into the advanced stages of the interrogation.[14]

Raj Kundra, one of the owners of the RR, was also accused of indulging in betting and other unethical activities, and along with Meiyappan, was prosecuted. The matter escalated, as the IPL, already reeling from a sting operation the previous year by a television network (India TV), had banned or suspended five domestic cricketers—T.P. Sudhindra was given a life ban, Shalabh Srivastava was given a five-year ban, and Mohnish Mishra, Amit Yadav and Abhinav Bali were each given a one-year suspension.[15] This, however, was at an entirely different level. The authorities invoked the Maharashtra Control of Organized Crime Act (MCOCA) against the three players and the twenty-three others arrested by them. The court too got into the act, and since the BCCI had made only a half-hearted attempt at putting together a probe to determine what had happened, in October the court appointed the Justice Mudgal Committee to probe the spot-fixing and illegal betting allegations. The committee pointed out serious irregularities and commission of unethical activities in its report submitted to the court. On the basis of this report, the court, in 2015, appointed the Justice Lodha Committee to analyse, recommend and, if necessary, propose directives towards rectifying any governance and/ or ethics gaps within the BCCI–IPL. In the meantime, due to the lacklustre effort made by the BCCI and the clear implication of conflicts of interest given Srinivasan's dual role, the court asked Srinivasan to step aside, and installed two interim officials—Shivlal Yadav to head the BCCI, and Sunil Gavaskar to head the IPL for the 2014 season. The spot-fixing scandal cost Srinivasan his BCCI presidency, and it may have cost the IPL its reputation. This will be analysed in detail in Chapter 2.

Between the Kochi fiasco and the spot-fixing scandal, Modi and Srinivasan lost their places in the BCCI, for the latter at least temporarily. The IPL was stuttering now, but there were other challenges to be faced as well. In August 2015, a potentially game-changing development came to light. For a change it wasn't related to an IPL scandal, although a familiar name was behind it. It hinted at a shake-up of cricket administration as the world knows it. Of course, it involved Modi.

A new world order

In August 2015, Modi was in the news for a development potentially more devastating for the BCCI than his rumoured dealings and scoops relating to the IPL. Modi unveiled his initial plans for a new world order in cricket, one which was to be closely linked to the International Olympic Committee (IOC), and therefore help cricket attain some semblance of credibility and global acceptability.[16] Global governing bodies in sports have not had a great run in the eyes of the public, with FIFA (Fédération Internationale de Football Association) continuing to be embroiled in scams, and Olympics not always emerging untainted; so affiliation with the IOC isn't necessarily a plaudit. But if anyone knows how to monetize and popularize the sport of cricket, it is Modi. If anyone also knows the Achilles heel of the BCCI it would be Modi. A new world order in cricket that is out to replace the ICC would normally be a pipe dream for anyone else, but if anyone has the nous and the drive to do it, it would likely be Modi.

The plan for this new world order is a parallel entity that organizes Test and T20 events, while dispensing altogether with the One Day format. It intends to play upon the discontent within the various cricketing nations that have not benefited from the power play in the International Cricket Council (ICC). The BCCI, England and Wales Cricket Board (ECB) and Cricket Australia (CA) together had staged a coup of sorts in January 2014 when the ICC approved a world order where these three boards became the Big Three in terms of revenues, influence and representation. Recognizing the importance of the three boards, the ICC agreed to hand over to them a greater proportion of the revenue, as well as the decision-making powers in terms of scheduling, finances, and overall governance. A five-member executive committee was created to act as a buffer between the executive board consisting of the heads of the ten Test-playing nations' national boards and the ICC committees. Of the five, three permanent representatives are the CA, the ECB and the BCCI. Eight of the ten full members voted in favour of this realignment, with Sri Lanka and Pakistan abstaining. The realignment was a controversial move, and clearly favoured a unilateral shift towards the three rainmakers. It may have created a chasm between the haves and have-nots, and left the door open for a parallel world order to emerge.[17]

It has been held against the BCCI that its interests are served frequently and disproportionately due to its financial clout, and also in terms of its representation at the ICC level. For quite some time now, outgoing BCCI presidents have landed prime positions in the ICC, possibly influencing decision-making that appears to be partial towards the BCCI from the perspective of the less favoured nations. Following the rise of the Big Three, Srinivasan was appointed the first-ever ICC chairman, in July 2014, for a two-year term. The duality of roles, where his position as president of the BCCI along with his new role at the ICC existed almost simultaneously, had raised many hackles. It is those who have felt wronged and ignored who may eventually tilt the balance towards a new world order that placates and woos them as opposed to the one-sided power game in the ICC where the Big Three had started calling all the shots. Modi, of course, would have been keen to take advantage of this situation. And believe it or not, he wouldn't have been the only one.

The Essel Group, whose foray into the Indian Cricket League (ICL) is mentioned later in this chapter, had also announced its plans for a parallel cricket order, and is said to be in the process of rolling it out soon. Initially, it was said that Essel and Modi were in it together, but both have quickly dismissed the connection. Indeed, given the distrust and enmity which would understandably exist between the two sides given the hostile nature of the tussle between the IPL and the ICL, it is unlikely that the two would align even if they both share a common enemy in the BCCI. So the BCCI and the ICC faced competition not just from Modi but also from Essel, and this could be a huge challenge given the credibility crisis that the existing cricket order had been facing. But then, in early 2016, at around the same time that the Justice Lodha Committee's recommendations were being reinforced by the Supreme Court, the BCCI took the somewhat surprising step of recommending the dissolution of the Big Three model at the ICC. This was an initiative led by the current BCCI president Shashank Manohar who had in late 2015 replaced Srinivasan as the chairman of the ICC, and will be discussed in detail in Chapter 7. Also discussed in greater detail in Chapter 7 will be the circumstances that led to Manohar's return to the presidentship of the BCCI in October 2015, and some of his initiatives towards improving the perception and administration of the board and the IPL.

On-pitch competition

Competition is something the IPL too now faces on a regular basis. At the time it started, the IPL was perhaps the only T20 league of some consequence. Today that is not at all the case. Domestic T20 leagues exist all over, the notable ones being Australia's Big Bash League, ECB's NatWest t20 Blast, the Caribbean Premier League, the Bangladesh Premier League, and now the Pakistan Super League (PSL). There is no shortage of T20 cricket now across the world, and these leagues mostly feature the same international superstars, especially those from the West Indies. No matter how good the quality of the cricket, it will eventually lead to saturation or the weeding out of less sustainable events. Already the Sri Lankan Premier League has been a casualty due to lack of sponsorship and organizational issues. Since the IPL's reliance on international players remains crucial, sharing the services of international T20 specialists is likely to be a limiting factor in the growth of the IPL from being a tournament to a proper league. Moreover, the issue of clashing schedules and the decision to exclude certain players from the IPL may render the scarcity of supply even more pronounced. Frequently, the ECB does not release players to play the IPL since there are domestic commitments or international fixtures around the time the IPL is conducted. Other boards too have fixtures during the IPL, so players are either completely unavailable or are unavailable for a sizeable part of the schedule. Team this up with the unofficial ban on players from Pakistan, and there is an all too apparent scarcity of supply waiting to happen. Banning the Pakistani players also means that some of the most exciting cricketers are not in the IPL fray, thereby robbing the event of some great rivalries; it is this omission that other T20 leagues can exploit since no other country has banned cricketers from Pakistan, even unofficially. The ban on Pakistani players is an unfortunate development that traces itself back to 2009, and may have everything to do with non-cricketing reasons. Things got worse in October 2015 when talks between the Pakistan Cricket Board (PCB) and the BCCI either got disrupted or ended in a stalemate; thus, the cricketing world's most lucrative and popular rivalry remains in limbo. Competing leagues from other governing bodies is a big challenge to the future of the IPL. The other challenge is the lack of sympathy or empathy that the BCCI and therefore the IPL receives from the rest of the world. It's difficult for a board and a league that have been as powerful, as wealthy and as autocratic as the two have been, to suddenly become sentimental favourites with those whom they have willingly wronged and over whom they have wielded the stick with an attitude bordering on impunity.

Besides the obvious, there is also a very real and troubling aspect regarding the IPL fixtures. At no point of time can there be a longer calendar for the IPL to ensure that it actually operates like a league and not as a tournament as it is currently structured. Also, since there is no minor league system in place, and the talent development agencies in India remain unstructured, the IPL may suffer a human capital supply crunch. After all that happened off-field leading up to 2015, the IPL does not need the challenges caused by cut-throat competition and the diminishing quality of its on-field product. More on this in Chapter 6.

Fallout of the spot-fixing scandal

Going back to the BCCI's problems. While Modi's frequent television interviews and sharing of information via social media have consistently disturbed the peace of mind of the BCCI–IPL establishment, there are many other issues the BCCI–IPL must face in the present tense. None is bigger than the unprecedented nature of reforms recommended by the Justice Lodha Committee in 2016, but the committee may not be done yet. There is a possibility of a third phase of analysis and recommendations with regard to players who could potentially have engaged in unethical activities and the punishment to be recommended for them.

That said, did the Supreme Court really want to get involved in cleaning up cricket? Almost certainly not. The number of opportunities given and the close calls survived by the BCCI should have sent off warning signals to the core group. For whatever reason, it did not. Left with little choice, the court decided to take matters into its own hands, and pledged its support to the people of India, the group most adversely affected by the state of the IPL.

More often than not, the board and the IPL have appeared to have missed the pulse of the public, and that of the judiciary, and it is this that has caused it much grief in recent years. Honestly, the board cannot afford to be so oblivious to the obvious, and what is obvious to everyone but the BCCI is that unless it shows remorse and initiative, the IPL may not last this decade.

To get a true picture of where the IPL began and what it hoped to achieve, we need to rewind to September 2007, when an idea that had been brewing in Modi's mind finally took shape through a surprising turn of events. No one, not even he, could have realized how big that idea would become so soon after it was implemented.

Not-so-humble beginnings: 2007

In September 2007, the IPL was launched with great fanfare and the timing couldn't have been better. The inaugural T20 World Cup had just commenced, and India had entered the tournament as rank underdogs, not having played any T20 cricket of note prior to the tournament.

In fact, ahead of this World Cup, India had played only a solitary T20 international, in December 2006 against South Africa. To everyone's surprise and delight, especially the BCCI's, M.S. Dhoni calmly marshalled his troops and pulled off a thrill-a-second win in the finals over a feisty Pakistan team, just twelve days after the announcement of the IPL's launch. A fairy-tale conclusion and a promising launch pad for the IPL was there to be exploited. Could there have been a better introduction to what was set to be a game-changing league? It seems almost providential that the IPL was unveiled at a time when almost 1.5 billion people had received a thrilling immersion course in all that T20 cricket could be. The irony, of course, was that the BCCI had shown virtually no interest in T20 cricket prior to the World Cup, given how profitable Tests and ODIs were proving to be in terms of broadcast revenues and sponsorships. India was also the only Test-playing nation that had voted against the promotion of T20 cricket at the ICC. But, with Modi leading the initiative, this was a golden opportunity that the BCCI was not going to let slip away. There was reason to hurry.

Before the first official correspondence about the IPL had made its way past the board, a rival league had already opened for business, in India, of all places. The Indian Cricket League, or the ICL as it was called, was actually the first-ever professional T20 cricket league. Conceptualized by the Essel Group with a pan-India plan and an in-house broadcasting arrangement on the Zee network, the ICL could have been the trailblazer all the way back in 2007. It had brought together some of the biggest names in cricket, including many of the fringe Indian players and in a business model where it mostly owned all of the teams and then assigned them to different cities and minority equity owners, it looked to have a bright future. At least, until the BCCI took it on and set up too daunting a challenge for it to overcome in the long run. In a matter of a couple of years, by virtue of sanctions, limited access to playing grounds, mass exits by players, and a slump in revenues, it folded, and soon the IPL was the last and only official cricket league standing. The individual aspects and details of the ICL are touched upon in various sections of this chapter.

Back in 2007–08, the ICL was in with a fighting chance to be a success. Set to launch shortly after the T20 World Cup, in an uncomplicated world the ICL would have cashed in on the Indian triumph. Instead, T20 cricket's sudden popularity in India highlighted how difficult it could be for an outsider such as the ICL to achieve success, and how easy it would be for the IPL to be a winner due to the 'official' status accorded to it by the ICC. The ICC maintained its stance of following the BCCI's position on the ICL throughout the existence of this unofficial league. Not only did this relegate the ICL to rebel status, but the BCCI had earlier used its leverage to make it even harder for the ICL to survive. It ensured that virtually no stadiums were available to the ICL for its matches; and secondly, it banned all players who played in the ICL from being eligible to play in domestic or international cricket. The banning of players was emulated by every other cricket board in the world, and the ICL faced the threat of a mass exodus of its players who feared that their international careers would be jeopardized. In late 2008, the ICL officials met two key BCCI officials in an effort to find a way to find some sort of middle ground and to allow the ICL to coexist with the IPL. The meeting turned out to be meaningless—lasting less than fifteen minutes and beginning with the premise of the ICL shutting shop— and the ICL officials fumed at the treatment meted out to them. Several months later, the ICC called a meeting of both parties so as to iron issues out. That too ended in a stalemate, as there never was a middle ground found. In 2009, there were even rumours of the ICL merging into the IPL as a franchise owner, but in all likelihood it was only a rumour. Eventually, the ICL was discontinued after two seasons amidst the exodus of players, inability to monetize the league, tardy salary payments to players, and perhaps due to certain controversies pertaining to match-fixing that plagued some of its cricketers.[18] Controversies that were not helped in any way by the overall lack of transparency. Pertinently, the match-fixing litigation is going on even today, with New Zealand's Chris Cairns at the centre of it all.[19]

In addition to marginalizing the competition, the original intent of the IPL was very different from the final product that was launched. Modelled on the US professional sports leagues with key elements from the English Premier League incorporated within it, it was positioned as a super-league of sorts, compressed in a forty-four day window that would showcase the best cricketers in the world. The goal was to build a club culture, and have the successful franchises invest in the sport, by having them commit to building stadiums. Also planned was a player draft rather than an auction, a process that is considered cleaner, fairer, and promoting parity across teams. The auction is analysed in detail in Chapter 5.

Structure and intent of the IPL

By December 2007, the original intent was no longer the vision of the BCCI–IPL. The franchises were no longer expected to create tangible infrastructure in the form of stadiums. Given the extremely short calendar of forty-four to seventy days at the most, it would not have been financially sustainable for the franchises to commit significant capital towards creating infrastructure. What this did prevent, however, was the basic tenet of creating value for teams. By entering into rental agreements with state cricket associations for franchises to play 'home' matches, the value of franchises in the IPL remained provisional and intangible. Till date, there is very little ownership of assets for teams in the IPL—even the intellectual property rights that give the teams exclusivity over team rights are co-owned with the BCCI–IPL, and therefore year-round monetizing or leveraging of team ownership is limited even today, and subject entirely to the discretion of the BCCI–IPL.

To ensure some excitement in player recruitment, and to incentivize star power, the Modi-led IPL abandoned the governance-friendly player draft, and replaced it with an auction where the minimum reserve price was guaranteed if the player was chosen by a team, and anything above it was an incentive bonus. The laissez-faire nature of the auction led to numerous loopholes and flouting of posted regulations and guidelines. Although none of the franchises has gone on record to express their displeasure at this easily manipulated process, one can understand if any of them felt the chagrin of consistently fishing in a depleted player pool year after year, as the player retentions piled up, and the good teams became better. One of the main reasons why the auction replaced the draft was because the BCCI was genuinely concerned that the high wages paid by the ICL would lead to many of the domestic and international players to migrate towards the rebel league.

To counter this, the BCCI wanted to ensure that the security of being allowed to play 'official cricket' would be further enhanced by higher wages, therefore making the ICL a far riskier proposition than it was prior to September 2007. By November 2007, the ICL had commenced its inaugural season at a few stadiums given to it by the Indian Railways and others—either private or controlled by sympathetic state governments. By all accounts, although unverified due to the opaque nature of the information provided by the promoters, the ICL had done reasonably well. Yes, the IPL had everything going its way—superior infrastructure, an elite player pool, and the support of the BCCI; but what it really needed more than anything else was a successful first season with the best players, and with franchise owners that were household names. It had its work cut out for it.

Transparency took a back seat in the IPL from very early on. The process of bidding for a franchise was mostly a secretive affair, and the honour of being given the right to own a team was a privilege extended to a few. The bids were intended to be sealed, and therefore secret. It is unclear whether the reason for this was one of these three: a) the excitement component would be heightened if the

final results were declared to everyone's surprise at one go;
b) the winning bids were for the most part already known
and to make it seem more competitive the BCCI wanted it
to appear as if there had been an actual protocol followed;
or c) Modi and the BCCI were actually wary of the base
reserve price not being met, and to avoid embarrassment
through a transparent process, chose instead to keep it
confidential, and therefore rectifiable if the franchise
auction didn't go according to plan.[20]

If there was a fourth reason, it remains unknown
even today. The fact is, none of the three reasons put
the BCCI or Modi in a particularly strong position, on
the eve of what was one of the most pivotal unveilings
in the history of modern cricket. As it turned out,
and for reasons best known to Modi and the IPL
governing council, the BCCI needn't have worried. The
pure economic monopoly that was created by the IPL
through barriers to entry, and a single product that no
other entity could match, proved to be a commodity
that exceeded expectations. The star power that joined
the club was mostly A-list, and the winning bid prices
for the franchises made news across the world. It was
unthinkable that a league in a format that had not even
existed for five years prior to the IPL was drawing bids
in excess of US$100 million at the time. The auction in
December had similarly created ripples across Europe
and Asia when players were 'bought' for as much as
US$1.5 million (Dhoni by the CSK) for just forty-four
days of competition. The ownership of the franchises
was a grey area, and even today it is unclear what the
value proposition for owning a team is. There were also

rumours—unsubstantiated, of course, that there was 'benami' ownership of the teams.[21]

The IPL was an amalgamation of all that at the time epitomized India—the glitz, the glamour, the corporate and entertainment behemoths, and the gushing masses. But beyond that, Modi and the larger-than-life franchise owners projected a reliance on sound business and strategic models which they felt would justify the exorbitant spends on a completely untried product.

The first season and the financial inside story: 2008

The timing of the first season was impeccable. Modi came across as an astoundingly astute businessman with an almost uncanny pulse on what the audience wanted. The dash of flair to this event was the various subplots among the owners, brand ambassadors and the players. The crossover effect and the mass appeal that the IPL had, made this appear less of a fad, and more of a phenomenon. Vijay Mallya, owner of Royal Challengers Bengaluru (RCB), and Shah Rukh Khan, co-owner of Kolkata Knight Riders, were India's George Steinbrenner, the high-profile owner of New York Yankees, and Roman Abramovich, the flamboyant owner of the English Premier League's Chelsea.

The revenue model was relatively straightforward, if not entirely thought through. The teams and the BCCI–IPL were both dreaming big, and the question was only about how to tide over the initial years. At the time, no one in the inner circle had any doubt that this was a phenomenon that would grow exponentially in the next decade. The only concern was about ensuring that the revenues were enough to sustain the league and the teams until gate receipts, merchandising, local sponsorships and other collaterals carried profits to the next dimension. Even the financial plan belied any pessimism, planning for a five-year stretch and then a ten-year re-evaluation and realignment of revenues. The chosen ones of the IPL could not possibly have predicted how difficult the initial years would be, given how well the tournament did in year one.

The revenues for the IPL and the franchisees came from three streams: media rights, sponsorships in the central or local pool, and gate receipts. The central pool consisted of sponsorships for the league as a whole, to be distributed between the IPL and the franchisees. The local pool consisted of sponsorships that each team managed to attract, of which the franchisee/team kept the entire amount. The franchisees incurred expenses in the form of team costs, player costs, marketing expenditure, stadium expenses, and miscellaneous spends such as in promotion, event management and administration.

In season one there were eight teams, but expansion plans were already in place. The initial declaration was that the first expansion would be in 2011, with the addition of one team. The next expansion was to be of an additional franchise in 2014, leading to a maximum of ten teams. The auction of the teams had brought US$724 million to the BCCI–IPL, nearly double the reserve price. Each franchisee owned the team in perpetuity, but was to make the payments in instalments over the next ten years. For example, the GMR Group was to pay the IPL US$ 8.4 million per year until 2018, as a franchising cost for

Delhi Daredevils (DD). In addition, each team planned its expenditure around US$ 6–8 million per year on acquiring players and other team personnel.[22] Each player had an initial three-year contract with the franchisee, and with the exception of an icon player, could be traded after the first year.

The franchisees had signed agreements with their home stadiums for the seven home matches that each team was to play, on agreed rates that averaged out to be approximately INR30 lakh per match. Each team was also expected to spend approximately US$3–4 million per year on marketing, promotion and event management costs.

The global media rights had been bought by the World Sports Group India (WSG) for a total of US$1.026 billion over ten years. A sum of US$108 million was to be spent by WSG on marketing, and the remaining US$918 million went into the IPL's central pool, of which US$316 million was to be paid for the period up to 2013, and US$608 million until 2018. The proceeds were to be divided between the IPL and the franchisees, where IPL's share was 20 per cent in the first five years, and increasing to 40 per cent from the sixth year onwards. The franchisees received 80 per cent until 2013, and 60 per cent from 2013 to 2018, with 80 per cent of the total being divided equally, and the remaining 20 per cent performance-based. Of this amount, a fixed percentage is subtracted from the franchisees' pool and goes towards the prize money.

In 2010, Sahara and Rendezvous Sports World bid astronomically for the Pune and Kochi franchises respectively. The two winning bids—US$370 million by Sahara for the Pune franchise, and US$333.33 million by Rendezvous Sports World consortium for the Kochi franchise—together generated nearly as much value (US$703.33 million) for the IPL as had the eight founding teams cumulatively (US$723.59 million) during the inaugural auction in 2008. The consensus was that the IPL had established itself as a stable revenue-generating entity.[23] Less than a year later, it all started to turn sour. Scandal hit the Kochi franchise, leading it to be terminated. Two years later, after a tenuous relationship with the board, Sahara, at the onset of a serious financial reversal across businesses, stepped back from ownership of the Pune franchise, and just like that, we were back to eight teams. It would be easy to blame controversy and scandal on the sudden and unexpected contraction of the seemingly unstoppable force that the IPL had become. But that begs the question: how and why did controversy arise in the first place, and that too, to the extent that the BCCI actually went ahead and risked embarrassment by terminating its two highest paying franchises? The answers are few, but there are some theories, and some explanations, analysed later in this book in Chapter 3.

The facilitation fee controversy

Like everything else with the IPL, the broadcast rights partners too experienced their share of drama and uncertainty. WSG had granted the broadcast rights of the IPL in India to Sony Entertainment Television (SET) for five years. In 2009, sensing the increasing value of media rights, the BCCI terminated the agreement, and WSG went to court. Here, it has to be mentioned that contracts with the BCCI are almost exclusively one-sided in its favour. The franchise agreements, sponsorship deals, and tellingly, the media rights agreement were no exception. Despite going to court, the negotiations between the IPL and WSG continued, and eventually, WSG's Mauritius entity, WSG Mauritius (WSGM), won the rights for an amount nearly double of what it had originally bid, now taking sole ownership of the rights for US$1.6 billion for nine years.[24] This, however, wasn't the end of it.

The SET, now called Multi Screen Media (MSM), was not willing to deal with WSGM any longer, and wanted instead to sign a contract directly with the IPL. Eventually, a deal was brokered, whereby MSM entered into a direct contract with the IPL for the India rights, and WSGM retained the international rights. There was a grey area here that eventually led to further drama in 2010. In order to ensure that WSGM was not the intermediary between MSM and the IPL, the parties entered into a contract on the side which gave WSGM INR 425 crore as a 'facilitation fee' for stepping away from the global rights contract with the IPL.[25] The only problem? The board had no knowledge of this at the time.

In 2010, it came to know that this deal had been struck. It took umbrage at the fact that money was paid to WSGM which the BCCI felt actually belonged to it since this was a domestic event owned by the board, and so the rights too were owned by it. In June 2010, the BCCI terminated the media rights agreement with WSGM, stating fraud and misrepresentation as regards the facilitation fee. MSM agreed to pay the fee to the board, and WSGM went to court. Arguments and counterarguments were made, but as

the courts deliberated, the BCCI went ahead and took out a
tender for media rights to certain territories outside India,
such as South Africa and Australia, seeking expressions of
interest for the period 2011–14.

Rumour has it that the controversy grew wings once
the BCCI had dispatched Modi; by linking him with the
financial irregularities in the media rights deal, the BCCI
was building a strong case to ensure his permanent exit
from the IPL. Internal politics aside, WSGM was not
amused, and once again moved court. And one more time,
it lost.

In 2014, however, the Supreme Court of India upheld
WSGM's right to get the matter arbitrated in Singapore
against the MSM as this was the dispute resolution
mechanism that the parties had agreed to in the accord
that they had signed with each other.[26] All said and
done, the IPL had in a short span of three years almost
doubled its revenues simply by leveraging the media rights
arrangement in its favour. But it didn't end there.[27] In 2014,
the ED began investigating the IPL for money laundering in
connection with the media rights agreement it had entered
into in 2009.

A component as large as the media rights deal masked
many other shortfalls in income that the IPL was facing
from other verticals failing to live up to initial projections.
Let's go back to the revenue model of the initial few years
of the IPL's existence. The central sponsorship deals were
for five years, and for the next ten years the IPL and the
franchisees were to divide the revenues in a 40–60 per
cent ratio, with the latter amount to be divided equally
among the franchisees. The sponsors included the DLF

as title sponsor, and associate/partner sponsors included Kingfisher, Hero Honda (now Hero MotoCorp), Pepsi, Citi, Vodafone and ITC. Each franchisee could have earned almost INR30 crore annually for the first five years. Additionally, the franchisees were entitled to keep all the revenue generated from the local pools, which included team title sponsorship, partner sponsors, licensing, merchandising (87.5 per cent of the revenues), stadium signage, as well as other forms of sponsorship at the team level. Franchisees had appearance rights over the players during the IPL dates, which were alluring to potential team sponsors who could use them for shooting advertisements and launching campaigns.

Gate receipts were projected as a significant source of future revenue despite the fact that the Indian audience had never really been exposed to a team loyalty culture; the exception being the loyalty shown to football teams in Kolkata, Goa, Kerala and the north-eastern states where tickets would be bought rather than received. At the time, the IPL was to receive 20 per cent of the total gate receipts from each franchisee, while the franchisee was to keep the rest. This was an area of concern for the future, since event managers and sponsors in India continued to dole out complimentary passes by the thousands; so a business model which included gate receipts among the projections was likely to be a flawed one. Recently, there have been efforts to decrease the number of passes and thus increase ticket sales; but the ticket prize is expensive by any standard. Perhaps this was a case of overcompensation in order to rectify the glitch, leaving the teams feeling compelled to up the ante for revenue avenues. Regardless, unless audited financials show otherwise, gate receipts remain a negative pecuniary externality. Seat sales are also performance dependent. Signage benefits for the league included stadium boards, of which the franchisees could receive a sixth of the total. Some would go to the main team sponsor, and the franchisee could sell the rights to the remaining boards at its discretion.

According to initial estimates, the franchises were expected to break even after the third year. 'Break even' was an enigmatic concept when it came to the IPL, but more on that later.

The only real challenge to owning a franchise in the IPL was the barrier to entry. Initially, despite the many figures thrown about and sky-high valuations, a consortium or individual bidder only needed to have around US$7–15 million to be up and running in the IPL. While that appears to be a lot of money for most Indians, for the kind of owners the IPL and Modi were courting, it was more or less pocket change. The IPL had generated so much interest even before it became operational that the sponsorships themselves ensured an inflow of around US$25–27 million annually for each franchise in the initial years, which was more than enough to run the show. And since there were no stringent requirements on ownership, speculation and eventually questionable ownership patterns led to future controversies that greatly undermined the reputation and growth of the IPL. It never should have been that way; and if, as was asserted by future BCCI officials, Modi was the one who rushed through all the diligences and processes, subverting accountability and governance in favour of revenues, there is no excuse for future BCCI administrations to allow this gross breach of basic processes at various junctures in the IPL's existence.

It was important for large-market franchises such as Delhi, Bengaluru and Mumbai to be competitive, successful, and create a large base of fans. It's a case similar to the big-money teams carrying the moneyball teams by virtue of generating higher revenues and volumes in bigger cities. Some North American leagues such as Major League Baseball follow this system where large-market, successful teams share revenues with the smaller-market teams to ensure balanced success and development. Perhaps this ought to have been the long-term plan for the IPL as well. What is baffling is how easy it would have been for the IPL to make a real difference in expanding and developing grass-roots cricket in India above and beyond merely monetizing it at the highest level. At no point was any effort made centrally to create a development league so as to farm and develop youngsters. Academies should have cropped up in every locality of India, inter-school tournaments should have been the norm, and for tweens and teens on the cusp of becoming full-time cricketers, there should have been training modules and multiple levels of district, state and national leagues that continued round the year. Instead, the skewed salaries that talented youngsters made through the IPL have only lowered the motivation to perform at the domestic level and grind it out.

The value proposition of the IPL

Let's face it—T20 cricket and the IPL were a brilliant idea, and the first indication that cricket was willing to adapt to the times. No sport other than cricket takes more than three hours per match/game. Constant viewing and a three-hour window meant IPL had hit the perfect formula, and immediately could compete with every global professional sport. ODIs (One Day Internationals) and Tests would have remained relevant to preserve the sanctity of cricket, but an exponential increase in T20 was all but preordained. The ICL had drafted the road map and blueprint but never had the opportunity and perhaps even the wherewithal to be the phenomenon that IPL became. But other cricket associations could; and competition across the world is now the norm in 2015. In 2015, it was easy to forget all the promise the IPL once held for Indian sports. It was touted as the greatest thing to happen to India, putting it on the global sports map. In its first season, it was labelled an unqualified success, and compared to the National Football League (NFL), the National Basketball Association (NBA) and the mighty English Premier League (EPL). For a league that was not even a year old to be compared with the leading professional sports leagues of the world, each of which had been around for fifty years or more, was of course premature, and also misguided, as we learnt with time. But at the time, it seemed feasible. The reason for this was that the IPL was a unique property in a sport dominated by governing bodies. The ICC, the BCCI, the ECB, CA and Cricket South Africa (CSA) each had a larger-than-usual role to play in the monetizing and commercialization of cricket. The BCCI, in particular, had witnessed a huge growth spurt in the decade preceding the IPL, due in large part to Modi. It could therefore have been forgiven for being somewhat arrogant, and allowing certain processes and verticals that were arguably questionable, for a simple reason—because it could. The IPL was a victim to, and a product of, the BCCI's complacency and belief that it was an invulnerable institution, one which could dictate the course of professional cricket for India and therefore the rest of the world. If one wonders why many of the processes and developments in the IPL transpired, the answer is simple—because the BCCI felt it could. If you wonder why the allotment of franchises were mired in secrecy, and the players were auctioned off like inanimate objects, again the answer is simple—because the board felt it could.

By 2008, the board was in a strong position, and it leveraged every inch of cricket's cross-sector popularity by wooing corporates, and convincing celebrities to be a part of the IPL. It was a winning initiative, packaging T20 cricket for the who's who of Indian society, and then convincing the passionate cricket fans of India to buy into this best-of-both-worlds scenario. Except that in its complacency, the BCCI forgot that it needed not only to make the IPL the melting pot of Indian society, and an entertainment extravaganza, but it also needed to focus on the two most important aspects of any sports league in the world. It needed to build tangible asset models for its franchises so that they could become independently viable and have sustainable revenue models. It also needed to ensure that the quality of cricket remained the best in the world, and that the focus of the Indian public was on cricket and not just the glitz and glamour. For that it needed to ensure that there was a level playing field for all the franchises, and a fair dissemination of star cricketers to each of the franchises. But through flawed and incomplete processes, the league became one of 'haves and have-nots', and that is when the IPL started to struggle.

Even today, the IPL's franchises have no clear tangible asset or revenue model, nor has the BCCI appeared to have done anything to guide the franchises towards doing so. In the absence of any evidence to the contrary, it would be fair to say that the blame for this lies to a large extent with the BCCI. And this lackadaisical approach is infuriating primarily because there have been so many opportunities for each process and revenue vertical to be improved, created, or supported at so many different junctures. Instead, evolution and progress were largely ignored, and the focus remained on the glamour and off-field ventures. Since the IPL began, the BCCI has gone through three presidents, and the IPL has gone through three leaders— be they commissioners, chairmen or interim directors of affairs. And not much has changed. The IPL has become an entertainment event interspersed with occasionally thrilling matches. The BCCI forgot or was unwilling to focus on its core strength and vital unique selling point; it digressed at multiple junctures, and in 2015, it was at the cusp of failing if it didn't completely recalibrate its priorities.

What the BCCI forgot to do was sell what really mattered, and today it is paying the price for this lapse. What the BCCI forgot to do was focus on something that was completely within its control and actually fell within its core competence as the apex body for the promotion and development of cricket. What the BCCI forgot to do was sell the sport. By selling and leveraging the sport of cricket, the BCCI would have grown the IPL, and the rest would have followed. But that didn't happen, though it so easily could have.

Initial competition and the ICL

If there is one thing the BCCI and Modi could be forgiven for doing, it is for announcing and launching the IPL's first season in a hurry. Modi and therefore the BCCI needed to leverage the success of the T20 World Cup victory before it faded from memory. It also needed to ensure that the Essel Group did not enjoy a free ride off the Indian team's success, and establish a first-mover advantage which would have been hard to dislodge. So, getting together all the pieces quickly was understandable. But what Modi and the BCCI needed to have done is ensure that systems either stood the test of time and scrutiny while the logistics were being finalized, or should have had an initial set-up period of one year during which time it could have got everything in place. The one-year term would have led to a permanent structure of the IPL with detailed and comprehensive systems, governance modules, rules, and revenue verticals; all this would have made the IPL both flexible and well managed. Once the first season concluded, the BCCI needed to run against time to make sure that unethical activities were not allowed to permeate the inner workings of the league, and it needed to self-regulate. It did not change anything, perhaps because it was in a unique monopoly position that at the time transcended market forces and the laws of the land, and was conceivably immune from any competition or setbacks. Eventually, things went wrong. Success begets attention and scrutiny, and corruptible links. The coming together of Indian society's manifold cultural powerhouses attracted the masses, but when the many different sectors and domains collided, the results were rarely pretty. And this amalgamation jeopardized not only the functioning and scope for improvement of the IPL, it also brought out the worst in society, and dealt many influential people and entities a blow that may take many of them a long time to recover from. The BCCI needed to know or learn just one thing to make the IPL a huge success. It needed to know *how* to sell the sport.

Where the IPL missed out

The IPL, by any objective measure, is not a huge success today in real terms. It could have been, but it is not. Let's look at what it could have been and how it fell short. For a sport as evolved and monetized as cricket has been for the last decade or more, the IPL started on a strong wicket. It started with a rush of interest from many corners to own a franchise for the first time in a sports league. The demand outweighed the supply, and it was the barrier to entry that gave the franchises initial value. All eight initial franchises got sold for more than their base price, and there were great expectations of return on investment. It was estimated, conservatively as the BCCI made it sound, that by 2018, each franchise would be self-sufficient with its own sustainable revenue verticals: local sponsors, sold-out matches, and demand for merchandising. None of these were tangible really, but given the exclusivity of ownership, the artificially created scarcity of supply was meant to add value to a franchise's brand.

The barrier to entry and the seemingly high ceiling that the IPL had for generating sponsorship and viewership in its initial years made the first expansion auction a runaway success. Only two of the franchises are not up for sale or are unscathed when it comes to scandal being attached to them.[28] Mumbai Indians (MI) and Kolkata Knight Riders appear to be the only two teams that haven't undergone a change of owners, been suspended or terminated, been in the market to be sold, or flirted with insolvency. The KKR, however, has faced its own share of controversy with the authorities. But from an ownership standpoint they have been relatively stable, and have remained competitive on-field as a team. Virtually every franchise has seen its share of strife. Today, no team in the IPL has a ready buyer who would pay the market price—the term being vague enough given there is no real way to value a team in the IPL. The operating costs have been steadily increasing, revenues at the local level have been decreasing, all other revenue streams have plateaued, and by the time the tenth season of the IPL comes around, the revenue share for the franchises from the central pool will decrease by a combined 20 per cent for the teams in accordance with the arrangement. Is the IPL a success? Yes it is, but in many ways it has really stagnated. The parity between teams is non-existent, the veracity of results is constantly questioned, the quality of the play is solid but nowhere close to exceptional, barring some rare occasions. As the costs have risen, it has led to higher ticket prices, and the watching of live IPL matches is less of a novelty now than it was when the league first started; so the willingness of the repeat fan to shell out a sizeable amount to watch a game in the stadium is likely to be limited and price-sensitive. The match timings also make the stadium experience far more difficult as the league is played during the onset of summer. It is the focus on making the IPL a general entertainment event that could also give it a shorter shelf life, and lead to a much quicker saturation point. Truth be told, it is a forty-five-day tournament pitting eight teams against each other in a round-robin format, with eventual qualifiers and a winner. A tournament champion has much less year-round value than would a league champion in the real sense.

Team loyalty is built over months, years, decades and even centuries. The team becomes part of a city's values, culture and attributes. The IPL doesn't do that with its short calendar and limited ability to assimilate with the city which it represents; the inability to engage with fans on a year-round basis hurts the league. Competition from other cricket boards' domestic T20 tournaments or leagues has also led to a flooding of the broadcast market, a dilution of the product offering, saturation, and reduced participation by international players. Already missing the Pakistan players since the first edition of the IPL, increasingly fewer English, Sri Lankan and Australian players now participate in the IPL for one reason or the other. As other leagues take off, and the relation of the various boards with the BCCI become strained, given the power the Indian board wields at the ICC, the IPL may risk being boycotted by some or several cricket boards, and become limited to being just a domestic tournament albeit a massive one, sprinkled with a smattering of international superstars. This will take the IPL away from its globalization agenda and its goal to be the most prestigious T20 league in the world.

The future needn't have been this uncertain. There have been so many tweaks that the IPL could have continued to provide a differentiated product that appeals to the masses. It could have gone downstream and created an year-round immersive development structure that involved the communities of the cities and towns in which the franchises were located. During the tournament, the focus could have been on how to add quality to the matches, rather than on how to make the experience more entertaining. A stale product is the first step to loss of brand value. The colour of one's cap or glowing stumps and bails do not on their own make a better product offering if the overall standard around the funk is average. Finding a way to give the audience the best and most intense matches based entirely on the quality of the competition would have been the solution. Getting the systems in place to limit corruption and thus ensure the veracity of the results would have been another. Providing for a longer schedule to make sure that as many matches as possible are played and the best teams move forward will also help the league. Widening the talent base and discovering exciting new players rather than flashes in the pan would make for thriving sport. And if the franchises attain tangible value, all the IPL stakeholders would work earnestly towards making the league a success.[29]

There has been a question mark over the leadership of the IPL. In the post-Lalit Modi era, there hasn't been a powerful and decisive leader who could make sweeping reforms. It could be argued that the BCCI is understandably wary of appointing a dominant personality to lead the league, but nonetheless, both longevity and decisiveness have evaded the IPL in recent years. The IPL is a constant target of the rumour mill and the accompanying speculation. It didn't need to be. And it doesn't need to be. Despite its alleged indiscretions and publicized egressions, the IPL can still turn it around and create value from the ground up. Even now, with its back against the wall and the judicial appointees wielding unprecedented power to alter the structure of the league and the board, conventional wisdom indicates that the BCCI will get yet another chance to self-regulate, and fix what is wrong. Conventional wisdom also indicates that the board could fritter away yet another chance to self-improve and to induce growth.

Take a step back and think about each year of the IPL, and try to find a single season that isn't marred by some controversy or the other, almost always related to off-field issues. Season one (2008) was the IPL vs ICL fracas. Season two (2009), the IPL had to move to South Africa at the eleventh hour. Season three (2010) saw the expansion of franchises to ten and then drama with Kochi Tuskers (KT) prior to signing the franchise agreement, and the issue of sweat equity. It was also the year the BCCI tried to terminate the RR and the KXIP. Season four (2011) saw the termination of the Kochi franchise. Season five (2012) witnessed the termination of the Deccan Chargers (DC) franchise, and the introduction of Sunrisers Hyderabad (SH). It saw the Pune franchise threaten to pull out, and it witnessed the first spot-fixing controversy in the IPL. Season six (2013) was a season that had more controversies than successes, with the spot-fixing scandal digging itself deep; this was also the year when the Pune Warriors (PW) withdrew. Season seven (2014) saw the first half of the IPL season move to the UAE because of national elections, and the growing role of the Supreme Court in the governance of the IPL. The court asked the president of the BCCI to step aside from official duties. Season eight (2015) demonstrated the vice-like grip that conflict of interest held over the IPL. This paved the way for the Justice Lodha Committee; then there were life bans on Meiyappan and Kundra, and the court continued to stop Srinivasan from playing a role in the BCCI. Moreover, there came the unprecedented decision to suspend two of the franchises. The year 2016 has already been a game changer and one where the judiciary appears set to ensure that no governance and ethics gaps will be tolerated in the BCCI–IPL going forward. These are just illustrative examples, but the fact is that each season has spawned more than a few controversies. Besides, there are the enemies that the IPL and its creators have made owing to the league's initial success. The devil lies in the details, and each passing day, murky particulars about the IPL come into the public domain. This book is about what went wrong, all that the IPL can still become and achieve, and all that the IPL should now do for its survival and viability.

2

Ugly Sledging: Spot-fixing 2013

The spot-fixing scandal of 2013 was the single most debilitating thing to happen to the BCCI–IPL. It shouldn't have come as a huge surprise given the 'open-office' feel that the IPL had since its inception. With the spot-fixing scandal came two major revelations about the BCCI–IPL: the porous governance and anti-corruption processes in place at the time, and the ills of conflict of interest. It led to the end of the board's autonomy and the beginning of heightened scrutiny through judicial intervention. It eroded the goodwill, reputation, brand and value of the IPL. The scandal was poorly handled by the BCCI, and it is perhaps because of this that the BCCI–IPL is in the kind of trouble it is in today. The spot-fixing scandal set a chain of events in motion that brought the extremely private BCCI–IPL into the public eye, exposing some of the deeper issues within the governance of cricket in India. The IPL depended heavily on the so-called synergies between entertainment, glamour, star power and on-field fireworks. The biggest problem with blitzing entertainment and power with a sporting event is that the chain of causal events becomes hard to track, and even harder to control. The intent to have a well-regulated and secure event was no doubt a priority of the BCCI–IPL. But then there was the inability to monitor the quantum of possible interactions between individuals for whom there should have been Chinese walls preventing any disclosure of confidential information, despite there being indications of all not being well. In forty-five to sixty days of frenetic activity quite a bit of the securitizing of information would have been lost in delegation or incomplete instructions from one individual or authority to another. It's unfortunate, but the IPL was the prime target for spot-fixing and illegal betting from the very beginning. With no affiliation to the ICC or even to domestic schedules, the IPL existed in isolation, and the results too existed in a vacuum. India is said to have one of the most active illegal betting industries, since gambling and betting are mostly illegal across the country with few and extremely restricted exceptions. Betting on cricket happens at every level, from friendly wagers to someone knowing someone who knows a bookie. It is not whether there was betting going on in the IPL; it was the extent of the impact the betting had on the results of the IPL itself that ought to have been the concern.

The closeness of owners to players and the proximity of players to their agents or friends at hotels or via phone or email meant that there was no perfect governance mechanism that could have helped the BCCI–IPL to prevent the infiltration of unethical activities. In the need to have the IPL matches and after-parties serve as one big melting pot for officials, players, important people, sponsors and, through the cracks, some unsavoury characters, a sieve for information and integrity was set in motion. How could it have been possible to monitor each and every player, personnel, employee, service provider, hotel employee, agent, vendor, etc., during their interactions day in and day out? The answer, of course, is that it isn't. If anything, it's a bigger surprise that spot-fixing or illegal gambling has not been more debilitating for the IPL than it has been thus far. It may sound ironic but it's the truth.

The gap between how much capped players made more than the domestic uncapped players meant that role players in IPL matches who had just the tournament to maximize their earnings were susceptible to seemingly minor infractions. There was the complete absence of any orientation or recourse for players who were approached by bookies or others during the initial seasons. In later seasons of the IPL, players were instructed to immediately report to their teams or the IPL if they were so approached by anyone. It might have been too late by then though.

The IPL in a short span of less than nine years since its inception has seen a lot more action off-field at least, than any other sports property, tournament or league in the history of sports. In an industry historically notorious for power plays, corruption, integrity lapses and other such maladies, the IPL compressed it all in a steep achievement curve that matches its unbelievable initial growth. Despite this achievement, there is one occurrence that, above all else in the IPL, turned it and the BCCI on its head, and put it in a situation that the two jointly or severally had never faced before. The spot-fixing scandal of 2013 was the Cretaceous–Tertiary (K/T) boundary for the BCCI–IPL, devastating to its governing members. It started innocuously enough in 2012 when some journeymen players were first caught accepting money for achieving desirable results in a sting operation by a Hindi news channel. No one could have possibly predicted that it would have been the precursor to the scandal of 2013.

It was 16 May 2013. Almost everything went wrong for the BCCI–IPL since that day. The Delhi Police arrested S. Sreesanth, Ankit Chavan and Ajit Chandila, all three players belonging to Rajasthan Royals. Also arrested were a slew of bookies, some of them said to have links to organized crime, and soon after that, a former RR player, Amit Singh, was also taken into custody. Sreesanth had already made news for the wrong reasons in the past due to his on-field antics and then been at the receiving end of 'slapgate' in 2008 when Harbhajan Singh slapped him after a contentious IPL match and was then suspended for an extended period while Sreesanth had been given a warning and let off. A talented bowler, it was Sreesanth's attitude that stopped him from enjoying a much more prolific career with the national team. Almost five years after 'slapgate', in April 2013, Sreesanth was in the news, again for the wrong reasons. He posted on Twitter that Harbhajan was a 'backstabber' and that the senior cricketer had not slapped him, but elbowed him. This was refuted by Justice Sudhir Nanavati who headed the inquiry committee probing the incident; he stated categorically that it was a backhanded slap. To add to Sreesanth's woes including his sub-par form, came unsubstantiated rumours that Rajasthan Royals' management had dropped him from the playing squad in the week leading up to the big exposé. However, the RR stated Sreesanth's omission had nothing to do with allegations of match-fixing.

It was Sreesanth's mercurial temperament that made it that much more easy for the Indian public to see him as a villain. The other accused were journeymen cricketers who had occasional success on the domestic circuit and sometimes in the IPL.[1]

The Delhi Police alleged that the three players had been found to have taken money for altering results during certain IPL matches. Sreesanth and others were said to be linked through their agents or acquaintances with bookies and/or organized crime syndicates. In exchange for money, the players had played a certain way that impacted the results in those matches. Phone recordings, WhatsApp messages, surveillance camera footage, emails and other communications were said to be in the authorities' possession that could incriminate the players and the bookies. The MCOCA was used to prosecute the players and the bookies since there was said to be a nexus between organized crime and the spot-fixing incident. In the entire machinery, the players never really stood a chance. The RR terminated the players' contracts and filed a first information report (FIR) against them. The BCCI followed suit and banned the players for life. The Delhi Police was confident that the links with the organized crime syndicates were provable, and the case against the players was built. The authorities invoked the Indian Penal Code (IPC) sections 420 (cheating) and 120-B (conspiracy) against the players.

The alleged scheme itself was elaborate. The players were asked to fix specific overs that they were bowling, and to allow a certain number of runs in the over. To ensure that the fixers and the bookies got the message, it was agreed that the bowlers would issue a signal before the over—such as moving their wristwatch, adjusting their jersey, or tucking their towel into their trousers. The Delhi Police had closely tracked three matches in particular where the Rajasthan Royals played different teams, and in each match although there were some omissions or miscommunication between the players and the fixers, what took place was reasonably close to the script. The amounts paid ranged from INR20 lakh to 60 lakh. Sreesanth's conduit was said to be his close friend and former player, Jiju Janardanan; he was also arrested. With thousands of hours of footage and a reasonably strong case in place, the players were well and truly in trouble.[2]

That at the time seemed to be that. The popular view was that the scandal would burn itself out and after the three players and some suspected bookies are punished, order would resume and the game would go on. All would be well once more with the BCCI and the IPL, and if anything, after a rather uninspiring season, at least people were starting to pay attention to the IPL once again. Complacency however had no time to set in this time. On 21 May 2013, a friend of some of the franchise owners and a celebrity in his own right, actor Vindu Dara Singh was taken into custody because of suspected links with bookies and organized crime syndicates. This was a body blow.

In the week that followed came the knockout punch. This was perhaps unfair because purely in the context of the spot-fixing scandal, there may have been little that the BCCI–IPL could have actually done. What it could however have done was put together a much more proactive, impartial effort at good faith to probe the spot-fixing scam; its failure to do so was critical. During his interrogation, Vindu is said to have confessed to placing bets on behalf of Meiyappan and others. The Mumbai Police felt that now they had enough reason to question Meiyappan, and so asked him to turn himself in for the inquiry. On 24 May, after interrogating Meiyappan, the Mumbai Police arrested him on charges ranging from betting and conspiracy to cheating. The previous day, the income tax department had initiated an inquiry into the illegality of the funds used for the spot-fixing payments, and into the hawala component to it. Pakistani umpire Asad Rauf had been removed around the same time by the ICC from its panel of umpires for the Champions Trophy, for his alleged links with the spot-fixing scandal. In September 2013, the Mumbai Police formally charged him with cheating, fraud and illegal betting, all charges that he refuted, but till date has not contested in the courts of Mumbai.[3] Immediately after Meiyappan's arrest, the CSK went into damage-control mode, and allowing this to happen was one of the BCCI–IPL's big mistakes. The CSK went on record to distance itself from Meiyappan's association with the franchise, as did Srinivasan. But the trail was littered with Twitter handles and television interviews which clearly stated that Meiyappan was 'team principal' and 'promoter' of the CSK. The CSK chose to ignore it. Meiyappan was merely a 'cricket enthusiast' and a supporter of the CSK, not the owner, the CSK asserted. In a country where cricket had once been religion, this blatant disregard for the Indian fans' intelligence triggered the downward slide of the IPL's credibility among the public. That led to the BCCI suspending Meiyappan on 26 May.

The wheels were turning, and the BCCI, helmed by Srinivasan, formed a three-member internal probe panel to assess the damage and allegations, especially those surrounding Meiyappan. On 28 May 2013, the BCCI–IPL set up the panel consisting of retired justices T. Jayaram Chouta and R. Balasubramanian, and the then BCCI secretary, Sanjay Jagdale. Things steadily went downhill from there. On 31 May, the panel lost a member when Jagdale resigned from his BCCI post; meanwhile, the BCCI treasurer, Ajay Shirke, also quit. The resignation was in protest against Srinivasan not stepping down from his post of president while the probe was going on. On 1 June, IPL Chairman Rajeev Shukla resigned. The next day, Srinivasan temporarily stepped aside, while Jagmohan Dalmiya stepped in as interim president.

On 5 June, there came another blow—the owner of Rajasthan Royals, Raj Kundra, was taken in for questioning by the Delhi Police. He was subsequently arrested. Now things were getting serious, and the Mumbai and Delhi Police were stepping up their offensive. On 10 June, Kundra was suspended by the BCCI. However, on 28 July, the two-member BCCI probe panel stated that Meiyappan and Kundra were not guilty. The blot on the BCCI's credibility quickly spread as investigations into the acts and omissions pertaining to the BCCI–IPL began.

Aditya Verma, the secretary of the Cricket Association of Bihar (CAB), approached the Bombay High Court asserting that the BCCI's probe panel was unconstitutional. He got the requisite relief he sought on 30 July when the high court declared the panel 'illegal and unconstitutional', given that the panel had not interacted with the authorities who were investigating the matter. It ordered the BCCI to appoint a new probe panel. On 5 August, the BCCI approached the Supreme Court in protest against the Bombay High Court's verdict. Two days later, the Supreme Court denied interim relief to the BCCI. However, on 7 October, the Supreme Court appointed the retired chief justice of Punjab and Haryana, Justice Mukul Mudgal, to assess the spot-fixing scandal—he was to lead a three-member committee that included Additional Solicitor General L. Nageshwar Rao and former cricket umpire and senior advocate Nilay Dutta. The Justice Mudgal Committee asked for four months to conduct its probe and report its initial findings. The committee was empanelled on the basis of it not having any vested interest in the outcome of the probe it would conduct; as an independent body, it was expected to provide its suggestions and observations in a report which was to be presented to the Supreme Court for further action. Meanwhile, Srinivasan had been allowed to contest the BCCI elections in September, but was not allowed to return to his post until the probe had concluded. It was also around this time that the CSK continued to distance itself from Meiyappan.

On 10 February 2014, the Justice Mudgal Committee submitted its report to the Supreme Court, and it didn't reflect well on the CSK or the BCCI. The committee's report was released in two volumes: the first containing the committee's findings and conclusion, and the second one had additional analysis and conclusions by Dutta. The conclusions and findings of the committee created a huge stir. This was for the first time that a formal body was alleging that there was illegality in matters concerning the BCCI and team ownership of the IPL. Many expressed serious concern over the supposed findings by the committee of unethical practices indulged in by cricketers both current and retired. Also worrying were the ongoing investigations surrounding player–agent relationships and questionable practices by team owners in the IPL.

The committee stated that the role of Meiyappan as a CSK official stood proved; so were the allegations against him of betting and passing on of information. But it stopped short of confirming the allegations of fixing, and advised further investigation. The committee further found that Meiyappan had violated numerous IPL-related codes and rules, and the owner of the team (even if Meiyappan was not an owner of the CSK) had failed to ensure that Meiyappan complied with certain BCCI- and IPL-related codes, operational rules and regulations. This had led to a violation of the IPL 'operational rules', and the IPL franchisee agreement. The committee also stated that the allegations of betting and spot-fixing against Kundra, as team owner of Jaipur IPL Cricket Private Limited, required further investigation.

The committee felt that the allegations of match-fixing and spot-fixing against the players from the Rajasthan Royals, if gauged on the basis of evidence provided by the Delhi Police, could lead to a criminal trial and that the punishment imposed on the players by the board was adequate. The punishment ranged from suspensions of varying periods to a life ban—in the case of Sreesanth. During the investigation, the committee came across allegations of sporting fraud against certain persons. Given the sensitive nature of the information, the committee presented this separately in a sealed envelope to the Supreme Court. This sealed envelope triggered rampant speculation on who had been named in the blacklist, so to speak. The Supreme Court, however, did not release the names. The sealed envelope contained thirteen names in total, including, it was rumoured, that of cricketers who had represented India. One name, in fact, was said to have been a member of the World Cup–winning team of 2011. When the court resumed the hearing on 7 March, the BCCI filed an affidavit accepting that Meiyappan was indeed an 'official' of the CSK but asserting how the actions of an individual should not adversely affect the CSK franchise. Court was then adjourned until 25 March.

And so it began. Over a series of hearings, the Supreme Court came down hard on the BCCI. The feeling one got was that it felt it had given the board and the IPL too many chances to self-regulate, and now the time had come to improve things through judicial intervention. On 25 March, the court asked Srinivasan to step aside from the BCCI to ensure that a probe was conducted fairly and objectively. This was the hearing where the court stated how it was 'nauseating' that Srinivasan had stayed at the helm of the BCCI all through the entire scandal. On 27 March, it appointed Sunil Gavaskar as the interim head of the IPL for its seventh edition in 2014, and Shivlal Yadav, a BCCI vice president, as the interim head in charge of all BCCI-related matters. The court reconfirmed its decision to remove Srinivasan from his position in the BCCI at its hearing on 16 April. It also ordered the probe on spot-fixing and illegal gambling to be conducted by the BCCI itself, rather than it being conducted by the court. The court also made reference to the contents of the sealed envelope, stating that Srinivasan's was one of the names mentioned in the committee's report. This was the first mention of what was contained in the sealed envelope, the contents of which remain unavailable even today for public review.

The BCCI had made a serious mistake initially when setting up a probe panel to assess the whole matter of spot-fixing in 2013 and now repeated that mistake once the Mudgal Committee submitted its findings. At the time what was needed, of course, was an independent panel to assess the situation objectively, given not only that the BCCI was involved directly with the IPL, but also because the CSK ownership was mostly perceived to be Srinivasan's. After its failed probe panel that worked during May–July 2013, the BCCI–IPL set up another inquiry committee which, incredibly, again failed the smell test. The BCCI's initial IPL probe panel was considered to be insufficient, inaccurate, and not conducted at arm's length. It had a chance to fix that this time. It didn't.

On 22 April, the BCCI submitted its nominees for the three-member probe panel: former cricketer and television commentator Ravi Shastri who was also a member of the IPL governing council, retired judge J.N. Patel, and former director of the Central Bureau of Investigation (CBI), R.K. Raghavan. The Cricket Association of Bihar (CAB) objected to this panel and the court too preferred to continue with the Mudgal Committee for a comprehensive probe into the scandal. The BCCI had objections to continuing with the committee, saying that its original conclusions were erroneous; but the court was past listening. The board now lost its fight against the court and the Mudgal Committee yet again. The Supreme Court then asked the committee to expand upon its initial observations and create a framework of its recommendations. It asked the committee to continue with its probe. The committee submitted an interim report at the end of August, and received a two-month extension by which to submit the final report. By June, Sourav Ganguly had also joined the committee by virtue of his expertise in cricket-related matters.

The final report was eventually submitted on 3 November. In the meantime, Srinivasan had received the permission of the court to contest and accept the ICC chairman's position, although he continued to request the court through 2014 to reconsider his eligibility to function as the BCCI president. The final report was even more damaging to the BCCI–IPL than the first had been. Most of the final report was kept sealed, and not released by the court for public review. Four of the thirteen names were revealed by the court, and they were already known: Kundra, Meiyappan, Srinivasan and Sundar Raman, the IPL's chief operating officer (COO). The committee found Kundra and Meiyappan to be guilty of betting; Srinivasan to be guilty of inaction in investigating allegations against an unnamed player (Srinivasan was found guilty of nothing else); and Raman, among other things, was said to have contacted a bookie eight times during a particular IPL season. The Mudgal Committee had seen enough to be convinced of the involvement of Kundra and Meiyappan. The BCCI, however, closed ranks and stood behind Srinivasan and Raman, opting to take no action against the latter. But the court was not amused with what it had seen, heard and read.

From mid-November 2014 to January 2015, there was a series of hearings before the Supreme Court, each increasingly more critical of the affairs of the BCCI–IPL. Srinivasan, in particular, was subjected to harsher criticism. Not realizing that his days as the chief of BCCI were for all intents and purposes over for the time being, he continued to negotiate through his lawyers the permutations and combinations that could help him maintain control of the BCCI, even if the IPL-related affairs were no longer part of his domain. On 21 November, he sought reinstatement as head of the BCCI. It was denied. Later, on 27 November, the court openly voiced its concern about allowing the CSK to continue participating in the IPL. This was the beginning of the conflict of interest controversy that began with the spot-fixing scandal and continued beyond it. With the focus now squarely on Srinivasan, the court extended the mandate of its scope, and decided on a much closer look at how the issue of conflict of interest was hurting the game of cricket. Then, on 9 December, it gave Srinivasan a choice—to choose between the CSK and the BCCI. In addition, on 10 December, it asked the BCCI to postpone its elections until 31 January 2015. The court also dismissed the BCCI's proposed four-point solution for punishing those found guilty by the Mudgal Committee, affirming that this could only be appropriately decided by an independent panel. On 17 December, the court once again criticized the prevalence of conflict of interest, but reserved its judgment on the spot-fixing scandal. By now, there were two distinct focus areas for the court: spot-fixing's impact on the integrity of cricket, and the prevalence of conflict of interest spoiling the sanctity of the IPL. I will explain and discuss the latter in Chapter 4, but for now let's continue with the spot-fixing component of the controversy.

On 22 January 2015, the Supreme Court ruled on the Mudgal Committee's report and findings. It now systematically began its intervention. After the Mudgal Committee submitted its recommendations to the Supreme Court, these now needed to be formalized through assessment and orders on the appropriate punishments. The court established a three-member panel headed by the former chief justice of India, Justice R.M. Lodha; the other two were former justices Ashok Bhan and R. Raveendran. This committee sought a time frame of six months to carry out its task, and on 14 July came up with its first landmark order. The scope of the committee's mandate was to rule on the punishments for those mentioned in the Mudgal Committee's final report. It also extended to the franchises themselves—the RR and the CSK.

In its report, the Justice Lodha Committee effectively put an end to the overarching autonomy of the BCCI and the insulated autarky of the IPL. Gone were the days of pussyfooting around the country's most popular sport. Now, in fact, the court and the committees were acting in a concise and surgical manner primarily to protect the sanctity of the sport, to assure the Indian fans, and to preserve the principles of natural justice. The Justice Lodha Committee went beyond the recommendations and placed a life ban on Meiyappan and Kundra from all cricketing activities, and also a ban of five years from having any connection with the BCCI. In part, due to the actions of their owners, the CSK and the RR were suspended from the IPL for two seasons. It didn't stop at that. The committee was also given the responsibility of establishing the guilt or innocence of the players mentioned in the Mudgal Committee's report.

The Lodha Committee sought more time before finalizing its orders. It also sought more time before opining on the punishment to be levied (if any) on Raman. Thirdly and most alarmingly for the BCCI, the committee would also recommend changes to the BCCI's constitution as well as to the governing documents of the BCCI–IPL. The submission of the second report on 4 January 2016 was the defining moment for cricket administration in India. The committee took almost six months in which to compile and submit its recommendations, but for many Indians who had been sceptical of how the board and the IPL would be treated, it was worth the wait. The report was comprehensive, well researched, balanced, and of course, unprecedented. It addressed what ailed cricket and the IPL, and it proposed solutions. Solutions that sought change in the very fabric of how the board and the IPL was run. The recommendations were far-reaching; as many of them are beyond the scope of the IPL and therefore of this book, I will attempt to briefly touch upon the most impactful ones.

The role of the committee was, as stated in the introduction of the committee's recommendation report, to 'recommend those changes in the Rules and Regulations of BCCI that will further the interest of the public at large in the sport of cricket, improve the ethical standards and discipline of the game, streamline and create efficiency in the management of the BCCI, provide accessibility and transparency, prevent conflicts of interest situations and eradicate political and commercial interference and abuse and create mechanisms for resolution of disputes and grievances.' The committee's approach to each issue, keeping in view the directions and the observations of the Supreme Court, was to find solutions by applying two specific tests; rather, seeking answers to two specific questions: whether this will benefit the game of cricket, and what does the Indian cricket fan want?

With the premise that the BCCI performs a public function, and keeping the interests of natural justice and the Indian fan at the forefront of the reforms, it was only to be expected that one of the major recommendations was to bring the board, and therefore the IPL, within the purview of the Right to Information Act, 2005 (RTI). Under this Act, a citizen of India has the right to seek information from a public authority, in this instance the BCCI. Coming under the purview of the RTI is something the board and the IPL has strongly protested in the past on the basis of the contention that both the board and the IPL are private bodies. This is a huge blow for the board and the league, although an expected one.

Of immediate impact to state associations and members of the BCCI were the next two recommendations: to limit the total tenure of a state association or board official to nine years and a cooling-off period after each three-year term. The age limit is recommended to be seventy, which would essentially spell the end of the administrative careers of stalwarts such as Srinivasan, Sharad Pawar and others.

Another landmark recommendation pertains to eliminating duality of roles—for example, within cricket administration a board member cannot also simultaneously hold a state association post. Then the committee has gone the extra mile to eliminate duality and conflict of interest by recommending that government officials and ministers must not be members of the board, and politicians be not associated with the state associations. The committee, however, stopped short of excluding all categories of politicians from cricket administration, including members of Parliament. I will discuss the need to separate the state (i.e. politics) from cricket administration in Chapter 4.

Next, the committee sought to instil a 'one-state, one-member, one-vote' system, meaning every state's association would have a vote in the BCCI, but only one association from each state would be given that privilege. For states like Maharashtra and Gujarat, this is problematic since each state has multiple associations with a vote in the BCCI. For states that did not have a vote in the BCCI, this is a positive move. Regardless, it is a move that will cause extensive resistance within the state associations. More on that in Chapter 7.

The committee recommended professionalizing cricket administration by hiring a chief executive officer (CEO) with management skills working closely with heads of key verticals to help streamline the processes and ensure that the board runs like a corporate entity. The committee also recommended an apex council for the board, which would essentially consist of nine members handling the governance of the BCCI, strategizing the development of the game, and above all, overseeing and monitoring the professional management of the BCCI on a day-to-day basis. The members would be the BCCI president (currently

Manohar), the sole vice president (the committee has also recommended reducing the number of vice presidents from five to one), the secretary, the joint secretary and the treasurer. The independent members ought to be two nominees (one man and one woman) from the players' association (recommended by the committee), another one from the comptroller and auditor general's (CAG) office so as to ensure financial transparency, and lastly, one elected representative from the board's general body.

On the IPL's governance, the committee emphasized the importance of representation across all stakeholders in the governing council in particular, and it recommended the structure to be as follows: a reduced number of nine members in total (as compared to the existing twelve members), including two representatives from the franchises (on a rotational basis), nominees of the players' association (also recommended by the committee to give a voice to cricketers), and a member nominated by the CAG's office. This, if I may add, is an excellent and much overdue suggestion.

On the issue of conflict of interest, the committee laid down norms to ensure that no direct or indirect, pecuniary or other conflict or appearance of such existed in the case of the stakeholders of the board and the IPL. The committee also recommended the appointment of an ethics officer who could administer the norms relating to conflict of interest.

The committee further recommended that two vital posts be created: an independent ombudsman who could help resolve grievances of member associations, administrators, players and members of the public; and an independent electoral officer to oversee the electoral process within the board and member associations as the case may be. It is important to point out here that Manohar had already created this post prior to the committee's report being submitted. (The role of the current ombudsman, Justice (retired) A.P. Shah, in resolving the conflict of interest issues has been discussed in some detail in Chapter 4.) The committee also recommended an independent electoral officer to oversee the electoral process within the board and member associations as the case may be.

One of the most controversial recommendations was to propose a stark reduction in advertising time slots during cricket matches so as to preserve the emotion of the game. What this will lead to is a significant reduction in the value of broadcast rights and advertising revenues for the board and for cricket. So this may need to be looked at more closely from a social cost–benefit analysis parameter to ensure that the board's and the IPL's profitability and long-term viability don't get adversely impacted.

One of the most futuristic recommendations was to legalize betting on sports in India, and I examine that in detail slightly later in this chapter.

For now, let's go back to the issue of the CSK and the RR at the time of the committee's first report. It has to be noted that the criminal charges against Meiyappan and Kundra were independent of this order, and the committee in its first report did not comment on whether the CSK and RR should be terminated by the BCCI–IPL. In February 2015, Kundra had already decided to offload his stake in Jaipur IPL Cricket Pvt. Ltd, the parent company of the RR.[4] The shares of India Cements fell by 6 per cent after the Justice Lodha Committee verdict was announced.[5] Real trouble had now come to the doors of the IPL, and things were starting to really shake up.

Lost in most of the back and forth between the BCCI–IPL and the court was the causal factor which triggered this entire breakdown. The players who were being prosecuted by the authorities for their role in the spot-fixing scandal continued to fight their battles. While exemplary punishment had been handed out to the players, and eventually to the franchises and the franchise owners, little was known at the time about the actual laws that governed the unique situation that the IPL had found itself in.

One of the biggest challenges that the spot-fixing scandal faced was the actual legal grounds on which to prosecute the alleged offenders. The laws around match-fixing, spot-fixing and illegal gambling were and continue to be extremely hazy, non-existent, or archaic. The MCOCA was always going to be a long shot, and in July 2015, the Delhi High Court found the players and bookies to be innocent of the charges made by the Delhi Police. This is being appealed against, but perhaps the MCOCA was never the best way forward given how difficult it is to prosecute hardened criminals, let alone misguided cricketers who in all fairness never intended to harm anyone in the first place. The invocation of the gambling law or the IPC too could be far-fetched in this instance. Let's now take a closer look at the laws used to prosecute the alleged offenders.

At the time the spot-fixing scandal broke in 2013, there were certain factors that needed to be taken into account for analysis of the enforceability of the charges. The first thing to establish was the category of the offender. There were five categories of potential offenders being scrutinized and possibly prosecuted: players accused of spot-fixing or match-fixing; umpires accused of altering their decisions based on an off-field understanding with a bookie or an organized crime syndicate; bookies who took illegal bets and also possibly engaged in spot-fixing/match-fixing; team officials with access to privileged and confidential information regarding team strategy, rosters, and an intimate equation with all personnel of the team; and the broader category of those who acted as facilitators or conduits for betting and spot-fixing/match fixing, as well as third parties who wagered bets, but were not bookies or player agents.

In the given framework, the enforceability of specific anti-corruption provisions of the law was non-existent. The same went for unethical behaviour either with or without a fiduciary responsibility to any third party; it was virtually impossible to prosecute and then get a conviction in India for spot-fixing, match-fixing, and even illegal betting. The threshold for proving guilt in a criminal case is almost impossibly high, especially given the magnitude of fixing an over in a match that has little relevance or patriotic value. The spot-fixing scandal was shocking and newsworthy, but more so from a scandal level of interest, not anything more egregious. The media had lapped it up, but when it came to specific statutes or provisions of the law that could be invoked in cases relating to sports, the prosecution would find it immensely difficult to have the charges upheld. This was one of the main reasons why not much was done in the case of previous match-fixing and spot-fixing episodes in India.

India is not alone in finding it difficult to ensure convictions for sporting fraud. When it comes to difficulty in prosecuting criminal charges in a court of law for sporting fraud, India has plenty of company. Even in sophisticated sports jurisdictions across the world, imprisonment for illegal betting, spot-fixing or even match-fixing hasn't been the norm. A stiff penalty and a lifetime ban from the sport for sportspersons found to be betting or fixing is the norm. A similar penalty is slapped on umpires who act unethically. Team officials, unless their actions lead to unjust enrichment, perjury, or irreparable harm to plaintiffs (shareholders or the public at large) who relied on the officials meeting their fiduciary responsibilities, usually face civil liability, and extended suspensions from the particular sport's governing body. Only when the offences extend beyond the playing field and enter the realm of morally reprehensible behaviour leading to more than just disappointment for the fan base, or when harm is caused to a plaintiff or a class of plaintiffs who, by relying on the honesty of the officials' behaviour, end up suffering financial losses, does the possibility of jail time or criminal convictions usually arise. The ongoing FIFA scandal, almost running parallel with the BCCI–IPL controversies, is a perfect example of acts and omissions that go beyond disappointment and minor infractions, leading towards criminal indictment.

In the spot-fixing scam, there were a few relevant provisions that frequently arose when exploring possible criminal charges against the offenders in any of the aforementioned five categories. First and foremost however, to invoke any of these charges, the prosecution needed a plaintiff, and an offence to have been committed. For players who allegedly engaged in spot-fixing or match-fixing, the plaintiff would have been the franchisee to which they were contracted. The remedy for the franchisee typically would have been contractual, which means seeking damages and perhaps exercising the ability to invoke a prolonged suspension from cricket. The RR terminated the contracts of all the players and filed an FIR against each of them. The authorities pursued criminal charges under the sections 120B and 420 of the IPC, and could possibly have extended them to section 409 (criminal breach of trust by a public servant/agent). This was a difficult case in which to get a conviction since proving conspiracy, cheating and criminal breach of trust by a public servant/agent in the case of players would prove to be quite high a threshold to meet. If however, improbable as it is, a conviction eventually results, the maximum possible sentence under section 420 would be imprisonment of up to seven years and a fine (compoundable by the person cheated, with the permission of the court). Under section 120B, it could be up to six months' imprisonment and a fine (non-compoundable). If convicted under section 409, the maximum sentence could be a lifetime or up to ten years in prison and a fine (non-compoundable).

For unethical activities by umpires or officials, the plaintiff would have been the league itself, as the umpires would be contracted to the central league and not individual teams. The punishment and sections however would perhaps be the same as those listed out above. In the case of Rauf, the charges were filed, and he was also banned by the ICC.

For bookies, the sections 420 and 120B of the IPC also came into play, and in addition, the Public Gambling Act, 1867. This, in particular, is an archaic law that really does not address the seriousness of the charges a bookie ought to typically face. It assumes that a physical 'gambling house' of yore still exists in modern times, and the punishment is based on that premise. One doesn't even know the leeway a prosecutor would have in order to prove that a gambling house in the twenty-first century could actually be a virtual one, and transactions conducted online or over the phone would meet the threshold of the Act. To seek a conviction under this Act, section 3 states that offenders are liable to a fine not exceeding 200 rupees, or to imprisonment of either description, as defined in the IPC for any term up to three months. The maximum penalty for bookies (or individuals who act as fixers) under sections 420 and 120B was perhaps the same as those for players and umpires. The plaintiff in this case, since betting is an illegal activity, could possibly have been an Indian cricket fan or the authorities themselves. It is important to realize however that betting on cricket matches may not even meet the criteria for inclusion under the Act, since section 12 states that any game requiring skill is not to be covered under the Act at all. Cricket has many detractors but even the IPL's biggest critics cannot deny that playing competitive cricket definitely requires skill.

The last category was team officials/owners, who acted in a capacity of fiduciary responsibility to all the stakeholders, and were privy to confidential and privileged information. If convicted, it's likely that section 409 of the IPC will be used, although it's difficult to envision a conviction under this section for a team owner in what is considered a league that entertains fans, as opposed to national duty representing one's country. But in terms of liability, a team official found to be in violation of his fiduciary responsibility, and engaging in activities such as sharing of confidential information, spot-fixing, match-fixing and betting on the team, could potentially be vulnerable. If the company which owns the team is a listed company and has shareholders, the shareholders may well be the plaintiffs, as could be the central league, or anyone else to whom the official or the team owed a fiduciary responsibility. If convicted under the IPC, the punishment is the same as I set out above for the players.

To summarize, there are five categories of transgressions that must be addressed: spot-fixing or match-fixing by players; umpires altering their decisions based on an understanding with a bookie; bookies taking bets illegally and also engaging in facilitating spot-fixing/match-fixing; betting by team officials with access to privileged and confidential information regarding team strategy and rosters, and the possible sharing of such information to outsiders; and lastly, individuals facilitating betting, fixing or other unethical activities that may alter the results of matches.

Barring the intervention of the courts, most stakeholders have limited or no recourse against the offenders. The cricket enthusiast today doesn't know which door to knock on against unethical activities in the IPL. As for the BCCI, it can't take any other action against erring players except to ban them from playing cricket at any level. The legal recourse for teams against the players is contractual—they can terminate contracts, and sue for damages. Sponsors who feel that the brand or goodwill of the IPL has been adversely impacted may be able to terminate their contracts, both as sponsors of teams that are being investigated, or at the central level due to the hit that the IPL has taken. Advertisers may be able to get out of their obligations if the league's goodwill is impacted, but their recourse will be through the broadcaster, not the league. The broadcaster, for its part, will only be able to terminate and seek damages if the central league is found in breach of its contract—a high threshold indeed. It remains this difficult to ensure that corruption or unethical activity is actionable.

Let's get back to the present and the catalysts. In July 2015, the players had been absolved of guilt by the Delhi High Court on the basis of there being insufficient evidence against them. This wasn't surprising given the criteria that needed to be met. The Indian legal system often takes a long time to conclusively decide on a matter—the framework and backlog is such that matters can take many years before being disposed of with finality. For a matter pertaining to sports and illegal betting or spot-fixing, which isn't actually dealt with in Indian law, it wasn't then surprising that the threshold hadn't been met, but more importantly, it also meant that the dismissal was likely to be only a brief respite from the litigation the cricketers were involved with. It wasn't also the end as far as the Delhi Police were concerned, and they continued to prosecute the matter further. Having been found innocent, the players, especially Sreesanth, began to plan their next step, namely a return to the cricketing fold. That, however, was not happening for them. In the euphoria of the moment, the players felt that since the courts had found the charges weak, it meant that all sanctions against them too would be immediately lifted. That wasn't at all the case. The BCCI wasn't budging, and shortly after the dismissal of the charges, it released a terse communication, and a correct one: 'Any disciplinary proceeding or decision taken by the BCCI is independent to *(sic)* any criminal proceeding and has no bearing. The decisions of the BCCI, based on its independent disciplinary action, shall remain unaltered.'[6] After the numerous stutter steps and indecisiveness that the board had demonstrated, this was a good move to take a first step towards restoring the integrity of cricket. The inability to find causes for action within the Indian legal framework is one of the biggest obstacles to integrity in sports. Since the legal route hadn't yielded a conclusive result from the board's perspective or that of the Delhi Polices, the board needed to restore its authority.

And in all honesty, the BCCI–IPL had every right to maintain the player bans irrespective of how the lawsuits progressed. One reason, of course, was that the charges against the players had not yet been bilaterally dismissed. The second reason is that there may still be another Justice Lodha Committee report on the players in the future, with no timeline as of now for when it is to be expected (if at all), and until now neither the Justice Mudgal Committee nor the Supreme Court has given the players a clean chit. If the Justice Lodha Committee does submit a report regarding players and unequivocally finds the players innocent of not just violating the statutes and laws, but also of the BCCI–IPL's anti-corruption codes and ethics codes of conduct, perhaps the BCCI could feel compelled to reconsider. Thirdly and crucially, the court verdict is actually irrelevant to the BCCI–IPL and actually not even binding on it from the perspective of disciplinary sanctions. For the BCCI–IPL, with respect to the reputation and sanctity of the game and the board's authority over it, the players have already done enough to bring the game into disrepute even if the court has felt otherwise. The BCCI is therefore justified in maintaining a status quo and keeping the players out of the fold. Perhaps later in time, some additional due process and a fair hearing to return to organized cricket could be provided to the players, but they shouldn't hold their breath just yet.

The way things unfolded, it was quite obvious that neither the existing legal framework nor the internal rules and regulations of the BCCI–IPL had taken into account that something like the spot-fixing scandal would arise. So if one were on the wrong side of the fence metaphorically, and were looking at doing something illegal along the lines of betting, gambling or fixing, there weren't many deterrents at the time which would have inhibited the prevalence of such activity. This is especially true if one looks at the revenues generated by illegal gambling and betting. The appetite for risk when the rewards were this high and the risk of getting prosecuted that low meant illegal betting and associated nefarious activities continued unhindered. This brings us to the proposed anti-fixing law that had been discussed with great fanfare and urgency all the way back in 2013 after the spot-fixing scandal first broke. The draft 'Prevention of Sporting Fraud' bill of 2013 would have been the solution if it had been drafted in a manner that covered most instances of sporting fraud. Despite sport in India being a state subject, for something as far-reaching and potentially harmful to sport in the country, central legislation in the national interest will be the inarguable solution.

In 2013, the anti-fixing bill was actively and aggressively discussed. At the time it appeared almost to be imminent, and in October that year, the first draft of the bill was placed in the public domain on the Ministry of Youth Affairs and Sports' website for public review and comments. However, it came at a time when the federal elections were looming, so it was pushed low on the priority list. Had it been a refined draft ready to be enacted, it might have seen the light of day. It was however a work-in-progress draft and it had quite a few omissions which needed to be addressed.

The Justice Lodha Committee belled a very controversial cat in its second report when it also suggested that sports betting in India should be legalized. This stems from a school of thought that had begun to make its ideas public all the way back in 2013, and this was the need to legalize betting in India so as to help generate tax revenues, and create a monitoring mechanism that is easier to track than it would be to track the current illegal network in India. Let's look at this recommendation in greater detail. Betting or gambling in India is a state subject, loosely governed by the federal Public Gambling Act of 1867, which, as I had mentioned earlier in this chapter, is obsolete and grossly inadequate. Most Indian states don't allow gambling or betting, including on lotteries.

The Justice Lodha Committee stated that it believes the legalizing of betting will help curtail the influence of unethical elements on the sport and its participants, including players and officials. The report drew a sharp distinction between betting and fixing, favouring the legalizing of the former and criminalizing the latter. One of the key safeguards in the committee's recommendation was to prohibit players, team officials, members and employees from betting. This, of course, was necessary, since betting by any of these categories of individuals would almost certainly cause lapses in integrity. But there's one gigantic piece of the puzzle which must be completed before betting can be legalized in India, and that is having a solid legislation in place, something which the committee too recognized when recommending a broad law that ensured the prevention of sporting fraud in India. But with it comes uncertainty and one that could trigger a state against Centre disagreement with regard to the applicability of a national law (i.e. the sports fraud law) on a state subject (gambling), and it is here where the recommendation will face challenges.

To get a broader perspective, let's look at how sports betting is treated across the world. Legalizing sports betting is a controversial topic anywhere in the world. In the United States, it is a state subject, and only a handful of states have legalized sports betting there. In Europe, it's more accepted, especially online betting, but there too it remains regulated. In India, the challenge will be the balance between accepting it as a necessary mechanism for helping eradicate unsavoury elements that threaten the credibility of sport and potentially impact national security, with the stigma that Indian society may attach to betting and/or gambling. Ironically, in the recommendations by the committee which aim to separate politics from sport, the issue of legalizing sports betting could become mired in political leveraging at the state level. A stated objective of legalizing betting is that it should help reduce the prevalence of black money making its way into the economy, and promoting nefarious activities.

As I had mentioned above, it is also expected to be a source of significant revenue for the government with some estimates around INR 10,000–12000 crore annually, while at the same time helping monitor and regulate sports-related activities and discrepancies. There are two direct positive effects: the first is creating a platform for transactions that are above board, either online or otherwise, where the casual sports bettor or hobbyist has an opportunity to bet on sports; the other is consolidation—if the legal platform attracts most of the sport-betting activity, it would automatically lead to the ease of monitoring and enforcing by the authorities.

The major risk is that certain individuals would prefer betting transactions through illegal black money channels, and could remain outside the regulating and monitoring mechanisms. These are also the likely catalysts for unethical activities, including spot-fixing and match-fixing; so a risk in the initial stages is that the attention of the enforcement agencies may be focused on monitoring activities on the legal platform provided, and not on the nefarious transactions.

For legal sports betting to be even marginally successful, it needs to be surrounded by internal and external enabling mechanisms, including the sports fraud legislation, getting the buy-in of states, strengthening the anti-corruption units in sports bodies, creating a strong communication network with the Central government's enforcement agencies, and cracking down on the parallel network of bookie-centric betting that won't be exterminated merely by legalizing betting as a whole. It's too early in the process to know whether the Supreme Court will push this recommendation forward, and if it does, whether it will seek to create a guidance framework for states to consider should they choose to legalize sports betting, or whether the court will merely issue a directive legalizing it outright. Speculating on this is premature at best, and it could be years before legal sports betting becomes a reality in India, if at all. Initial indicators have not shown any states using the recommendation yet to legalize sports betting, but then again it's very early going just now.

A sports fraud law on the other hand is important not only to restore credibility but also to set up a competent monitoring and punishment mechanism in the absence of a viable alternative. We've seen how the legal system is limited when it comes to establishing and punishing unethical activity in sports; this is in large part due to the dichotomous nature of the laws under which the erring individuals or entities are prosecuted. The MCOCA is too stringent, the Public Gambling Act is obsolete and incoherent, and the IPC doesn't adequately cover the situations faced in sports. Also, the reliance on the BCCI–IPL and its anti-corruption codes and units is not likely to sufficiently bridge the gap, given the credibility shortfalls each faces in the current environment. This may be an undeserved knock on the BCCI–IPL but currently that's how the cookie is crumbling.

The sports fraud law should clearly demarcate causation and punishment, as well as a tangible course of action against potential offenders. It will also be a deterrent to likely offenders who would now be aware that unethical activity in sports would be tried and punished. Further, it would help to ensure consistency across India in resolving unethical activity in sports. It would also prevent situations where in the absence of a Central law, perpetrators have the option to migrate to states where such laws either don't exist or are less stringent. This is a real risk in terms of enforcement of a sports fraud law on a state-by-state basis. The Centre seems to have recognized this, and there are numerous sources hinting at the imminent announcement of a sports fraud law by 2016, although there hasn't been much apparent movement on this yet. It's late, yes, but not too late yet. Having legislation such as this will ensure the adequate redressal of the issues being faced in the ongoing BCCI–IPL controversies. It will also help to effectively and expeditiously punish or absolve those accused of unethical activity in sports. An inbuilt inhibitor in the legal framework for sports fraud would be a good thing.

A word of caution though—the final sports fraud legislation will need to be drafted very carefully, because there is always the risk of over-regulation, and the removal of the prospect of human error or skill limitations must be taken into consideration before enacting this. Among other aspects, the scope of the legislation should be limited to off-field collusion or understandings that lead to an altering of the on-field results or performances; and, to maintaining an arm's-length relationship with all activities that lead to a possible conflict of interest between the principals and the agents. Also, the legislation should allow plaintiffs who can prove that they personally have been harmed by the actions of the offender, and not merely invoke a provision for 'greater public good' that sometimes accompanies frivolous PILs (public interest litigations). The sports fraud legislation was needed as recently as yesterday, so one can only hope it is acted upon urgently—hopefully even before season nine or sometime in early 2016.

By now we know that spot-fixing scandals can be debilitating to nascent sports properties such as the IPL. It would be comforting to the BCCI–IPL to also know that established sports leagues too have risked failure and closure due to unethical activities within them. The IPL does need to right the ship and steer the course that is straight and decisive, and there is the example of organized baseball that immediately comes to mind.

North America's Major League Baseball was reeling from the Black Sox scandal of 1919, when eight players from Chicago White Sox essentially 'threw' the World Series, deliberately losing to Cincinnati Reds in baseball's version of match-fixing. Landis, a US federal judge, accepted the appointment as the first commissioner of baseball with sole and unlimited authority to act in the 'best interests' of the sport. Determined to maintain the integrity of the game, he banned the eight White Sox players involved in the scandal in one of his first acts as commissioner. What followed was a reign of 'terror', where he purged baseball of all its vices. He exercised his authority with an iron fist, and ensured that the integrity of baseball was restored. His actions are credited with cleaning up the sport in the twenty-plus years he remained the commissioner. During his tenure, he also banned a player for theft and receiving stolen property; another for suggesting he would leave his club to ensure his own team lost the play-offs; a player and a coach for attempting to bribe an opposing player; and a president of a baseball team for betting on baseball games. The internal 'commissioner' or 'chairman' construct in the IPL hasn't worked well. If the BCCI–IPL is really committed to improving its reputation and run a tight and corruption-free ship, it could perhaps consider bringing in an external and respected individual with a stainless reputation to either run the IPL or monitor it closely for the next few seasons as it brings systems back on track. Names that come to mind include both the retired justices who have either led the probe, Justice Mudgal, or led the enforcement committee, Justice Lodha. This could be radical but it should at some point be contemplated.

Although the BCCI had been at the wrong end of many PILs in the past, the number of court cases involving the BCCI–IPL increased dramatically in the aftermath of the scandal. Almost each week it appeared as if the BCCI–IPL was in court. Some were matters that had been ongoing and coincidentally cropped up around the same time. Others were likely by those scenting some sort of vulnerability at the BCCI's and the IPL's end. Perhaps this was only to be expected for an entity that had been as impenetrable and impregnable as the board had been—any chink in its armour was likely to be exploited by the many who felt that the board was an entity that required outside intervention to clean its cupboards.

Truth be told, the BCCI and the IPL had probably not made too many friends in the past, and there were many who would have taken advantage of the situation. Other factors that could have played a part were the willingness of courts across India to hear matters pertaining to cricket, and the expediency with which these were being ruled on. Also to be considered is the fact that the IPL had set into motion many litigable actions, given the overall lack or lapse of governance, and therefore, although we were paying more attention to the litigation involving the BCCI–IPL, it could perhaps have been a normal volume of lawsuits with which it was faced. Also, it is important to note that two of its most belligerent former officials were regularly knocking down the doors of the BCCI in an effort to gain influence once more within the hallowed precincts of the board. Back in 2009, one could never have imagined that the two most likely to be in control of Indian cricket, at least until 2020, would today be battling the BCCI tooth and nail to get a toehold back.

Modi and Srinivasan are reluctant colleagues in the fight against exclusion, and from the looks of it, are caught in a losing fight. Whatever the reason, two and a half years after the spot-fixing scandal first broke out, the BCCI–IPL is still swarmed by litigation, and it appears to continue unabated. The biggest fallout of the spot-fixing scandal was going to be the eventual involvement and intervention by the Supreme Court into the workings of the BCCI–IPL. And that's how it came to pass. Read on for how conflict of interest became the most prevalent point of the entire spot-fixing scandal and about the impact of the Justice Lodha Committee's order suspending the CSK and the RR, and preventing Srinivasan from returning to the fold of the BCCI.

3

It's All about the Teams

Given the BCCI's complete control over cricket, and the IPL captivating the new generation of cricketers and fans, for the first few seasons everyone wanted to be a part of this great Indian roadshow. Between sponsors, broadcasters, players and personnel, there was a constant rush to be involved in some capacity with the IPL. In a monopolistic set-up where the IPL was the most coveted sports property in Asia and the fastest rising professional sports league in the world, there was a bull rush to be a member of the extremely expensive and exclusive association—that of a franchise. For the first eight franchises, the BCCI–IPL picked and chose across a wide range of bids. By 2010, the ownership of an IPL team meant unlimited branding, screen time, and as was promised, steeply rising valuations. Initially in 2008, enough people wanted to be a part of the IPL franchisee club, but many were still wary. In 2010, almost everyone considered vying for ownership, and the most aggressive ones succeeded. By 2013, the dream of being a team owner in the IPL seemed far more tinged with risk, and by 2015, even those who had aggressively pitched for ownership in the past had withdrawn in the light of scandals and sanctions.

In total, eleven different teams have participated in the IPL, and for a while in the middle there were just six lined up to compete in IPL 2016. Yes, the CSK and the RR have only been temporarily sidelined, but in a short span of eight years, nearly half the teams have faced permanent or extended exclusion. In total, these are the past and/or present teams in the IPL: Royal Challengers Bangalore (playing), Chennai Super Kings (suspended), Delhi Daredevils (playing), Deccan Chargers (terminated), Kings XI Punjab (playing), Kochi Tuskers (terminated), Kolkata Knight Riders (playing), Mumbai Indians (playing), Pune Warriors (terminated), Rajasthan Royals (suspended) and Sunrisers Hyderabad (playing). Apart from the currently terminated and suspended franchises, Kings XI Punjab had been terminated in 2010 as had Rajasthan Royals, but both won their appeals and were reinstated by the courts.[1] This means that of the eight franchises today, only four have been with the IPL since its inception. Even for a property that is as exciting and thrill-a-minute as the IPL, the franchises have often run into trouble.

If the two biggest scandals to rock the IPL were the spot-fixing and conflict of interest controversies, it is the franchise group that has faced the most strife in the whole set-up. Besides the obvious struggle with the IPL governing council and each other, ownership of teams hasn't always been rewarding. There have been a number of areas where unnecessary challenges have arisen. A lack of control over the scheduling and venue of the various editions of the IPL has been the first test. The inability to receive consistent and beneficial platforms for revenue or team strengthening has been another. While the owner finds it difficult to monitor both the team and its officials, he is also vulnerable to the acts or omissions of those who knowingly flout laws. To have expectations of multiple revenue verticals and the freedom to expand these verticals through year-round initiatives would have been encouraging. But to then be unable to avail of the perks either because of lack of opportunity and experience or due to the sagging reputation of the parent association and the league itself would doubtless be discouraging. More than anything else, the most deflating part of being a team owner is the fluidity of ownership and the fact that liquidity is virtually non-existent. The gradual reality that like much of the IPL's long-term growth, not a whole lot has come to fruition in terms of returns on investment must be extremely disheartening for the franchises that have been in it for the long haul.

The BCCI did put together a great show from day one of the IPL's launch. The sponsorship deals, including the broadcast rights agreement arrived at even before the IPL began, put significantly less pressure on the team owners than would have been the case for any other first-year sports league. With constant sources of revenue and a certain degree of hand-holding, initially revenue was probably not a source of pressure. If the BCCI–IPL can be blamed for anything when it comes to the franchises, it is that it behaved inconsistently and too rigidly with them. By 2015, so much had gone wrong for many of the franchises that it was hard to imagine that these entities and individuals actually joined the IPL by choice. Now, they may find it costly to opt out.

Owning a franchise or team in the IPL was meant to be a privilege and an honour. It was certainly treated as such in 2008 and then again in 2010. With mostly assured revenues from the central pool and the opportunity to leverage team sponsorship deals, owning a franchise was seen not only as an outstanding branding opportunity, but also as a future tradable asset. Its economic model was simple: scarcity of supply offset by excess demand, barriers to entry or competition, and a stake in the future format of the most popular sport in South Asia. Barring the high of the 2010 IPL expansion, the promised valuations have only been pipe dreams, and the expansion, of course, got busted. Since 2011, many of the franchises have been seeking a partial or complete sale of their teams, while the equity holders have been keen to opt out. Most of this can be attributed to the struggles of the franchise owners in their non-cricket-related businesses. But that's not the only reason. Increasingly, it has become more and more expensive to own and operate an IPL team, and with reduced investor confidence, the risk parameters have skyrocketed. Add to that the simple fact that none of the IPL franchises have gained value in actual terms; then comes the realization that being a team owner is not at all peachy.[2]

When assessing the franchisee experience and overall incidents, let's start from the IPL's high. In 2010, the IPL was about to enter the next phase of its success story. Investments in many of the teams were imminent. The expansion to ten franchises had been a huge success where potential franchises bid sky-high for the right to own a team. At that time, the preposterous amounts bid for the Pune and Kochi teams made the world sit up and take notice. The IPL was looking like a phenomenon rather than a fad, and the team owners of the initial editions were perceived to be sitting on gold mines. Eventually, this turned out to be a bubble valuation that many had predicted, but in 2010, few actually thought it would come to be. If ever there was a peak that the IPL had reached in its seven seasons, the 2010 season was it. Despite the self-imposed litigation that led to its attempting to terminate the RR and the KXIP earlier that year, with the amount of interest the expansion auction generated, one felt it was almost invulnerable.

As I had mentioned earlier, the two winning bids of the 2010 franchise auction had generated a significant premium for the league, over the inaugural franchise values. This was, of course, remarkable and at the time there didn't seem to be a ceiling on the league's potential. The two new teams were expected to spend in excess of US$50 million a year to own a team, significantly more than it had cost the original eight teams to operate. Had this cost increase been accompanied by a corresponding increase in revenues, this would not have been nearly as much of a concern than if the reality hadn't been exactly the opposite. The expansion meant that the proportion of the central revenue pool that each team received was reduced from 7.5 per cent to 6 per cent. Unless the future revenues that the league received as part of the central revenue pool increased exponentially, the costs would continue to increase, while the revenues wouldn't. Since neither of the two new franchises made it past 2013, the issue of diluted revenues never really became a major bone of contention. But given time, it would have.

Current status of the IPL franchises

By 2015, most of the franchises with the exception of a couple have been involved with or linked to a scandal of some sort. Of the eleven owners in total, taking into account the two owners of the Hyderabad franchise, let's have a look at what the owners or teams have done in recent years. Kochi and Pune will be discussed later in this chapter, but here it has to be mentioned in passing that their promoters have been caught up in tragedy or prosecuted in non-cricket-related endeavours. The challenges and issues with the CSK and the RR are discussed at length throughout the book and the valuation controversies of the CSK will be discussed shortly.

The KKR has been a successful team but its nexus (whether the rumours are true or not) with Modi has attracted speculation. It was also one of the first franchises to be pulled up by the ED for alleged foreign exchange violations, back in 2008. This taint still dogs the ownership, and as recently as May and end-October 2015, Shah Rukh Khan as co-owner of the KKR was summoned by the ED to explain the apparent undervaluing of its shares in a 2008 transfer to a company in Mauritius. The KKR, operating under the company Kolkata Knight Riders Sports Private Limited, is officially co-owned by Khan, actress Juhi Chawla and her husband Jay Mehta. It is perceived to be one of the better governed franchises with a professional management team.

The RCB is likely for sale if anyone will buy it, but the owners are not on the same page. Diageo, the parent company, is adamant that it wants to exit, while Vijay Mallya, the face of the team and of United Breweries, is clearly not in agreement. Deccan Chargers was terminated by the BCCI–IPL, while its parent company, the Deccan Chronicle group, is today struggling for survival. Sunrisers Hyderabad was the Chargers' replacement and kept the team in Hyderabad, albeit rebranded. A moderately successful franchise, it's the ownership of the team that has been at the centre of controversy in recent months. The Sun Group and its main promoters, the Marans, have found themselves embroiled in non-cricket-related controversies, some of which escalated in 2015. At the centre of a CBI probe into the Aircel–Maxis deal and allegations of fraud,[3] the embattled Sun Group has not yet addressed any concerns about the future of its team, but from a business sense, an IPL franchise is by far going to be the easiest one to part with if the going gets tough. The price it would get if the team is sold is another matter altogether. The GMR Group has been in the market to sell Daredevils for some time now, and rumours about potential buyers do come up periodically. Talks in 2013 with steel magnate and sports investor Lakshmi Mittal were widely reported as were recent talks with the Kolkata-based RP-Sanjiv Goenka Group, among others. That said, nothing rosy has happened for the team, and that includes its on-field woes. Of the original eight franchises, Daredevils are the only ones to have not featured in an IPL final. A peaks-and-troughs kind of performance in the eight seasons of the IPL has led them to make drastic decisions and they depend heavily on the auction for quick results. That has not happened, and the DD has been one of the worst performers in the IPL despite the massive payout to Yuvraj Singh, Angelo Mathews and others as recently as 2015 (discussed in Chapter 5). For GMR, it has been a problematic stint with the IPL. Making the brave decision of owning a team in Delhi was always going to be fraught with logistical problems. The reasoning behind the move was that since GMR did not have a strong presence in the north or in fact anywhere outside Hyderabad at the time, owning a Delhi team would be a major public relations boost. It was also granted the rights to develop the new international airport in Delhi, the Delhi International Airport Limited (DIAL) project. Therefore, its connection with Delhi was set to increase manifold. By 2013 however, GMR seemed to have had enough, given that it reportedly was one of the most indebted companies in India; going by that situation, a luxury such as running a sports team in the IPL was obviously going to be the most dispensable. Except, of course, that the IPL teams have proven to be illiquid and misleading in terms of valuation projections, so the quest for a buyer may be a difficult one.

The KXIP has just recently been linked to Lalit Modi during the course of a rumoured sale of the franchise. If that's not enough, the KXIP has in the past been terminated, and due to the high profiles of its most visible owners, is frequently in the news. Preity Zinta was recently in the news when a leading daily quoted sources within the board as saying that Zinta had shared with the governing council that players in her team had probably fixed matches. But Zinta strongly condemned the story and the statements attributed to her.[4]

Barring some incidental auction benefits and compromises, the MI would today arguably be considered the most viable franchise in the IPL. Stability of ownership and the machinery of a leading corporate brings with it many benefits. But it's not that the MI has been trouble-proof—there has been the 'slapgate' incident and another one involving the South African cheerleader Gabriella Pasqualotto (she was later sacked).

The transparency of ownership in the IPL or the lack thereof has always garnered a lot of attention, but things came to a head when the equity ownership of the Kochi franchise came under the microscope in 2010. The Kochi franchise was star-crossed from the very beginning. Despite being an underdog in the high-value stakes of 2010, it emerged as the Cinderella story that fast became a nightmare for everyone involved with it. There were the questions that surrounded its ownership, the very public spat between Modi and Tharoor, breaches of confidentiality, the inability of the consortium to put together the funds for the franchise fee—all of this led to threats of termination, and finally, termination itself. It was brutal and it took a toll on a number of high-profile individuals. In its short stint with the IPL the Kochi franchise caused all kinds of havoc.[5] It cost a Cabinet minister his portfolio, it led to the exit of Modi, and there was an extended dispute resolution process which recently went in favour of the

Kochi franchise. Its future course of action may include a return to the IPL. Full circle? Not quite, but definitely a victory for the Kochi ownership.

The Kochi story was actually an opportunity lost for the owners, the state of Kerala and the IPL. Kerala was one of the few states left where cricket had not yet reached its potential, in large part due to the popularity of football. This was possibly because of the lack of cricketing superstars from there, Sreesanth included. Even in other football-crazy states, such as West Bengal, the emergence of an icon can change the entire dynamic—Sourav Ganguly did plenty to popularize the sport in the football capital of India. With the exception of the north-east where organizing cricket tourneys would be a task in itself, there were few bastions left. Kerala was one of them. Used to a league format thanks to football's popularity, it may not have been hard to establish a rabid fan base for Tuskers, thus obviating the need to instil team loyalty principles, or to try and promote gate revenue. Team loyalty could have led to merchandise sales, and the creation of a lucrative brand—the team itself. In its first run, there were too many off-field digressions. It's unfortunate because Kochi could actually have been a pioneer for league sports in India— even constructing a stadium was a possibility. As it turned out, the Kochi franchise was a pipe dream all along, and its demise also put on temporary hold the debate on conflict of interest, and diligence on ownership.

I had earlier mentioned a recent silver lining for the Kochi franchise. The BCCI–IPL faced legal action against it from the expelled Kochi franchise for which both parties agreed to go for arbitration. Missing from this latter episode was the initial set of individuals who had been in the news and at the epicentre of the controversy. Both Tharoor and Modi were no longer involved at this juncture. The arbitrator, former Chief Justice of India R.C. Lahoti, decided in favour of the Kochi franchise, and awarded damages of INR550 crore to it.[6] This was to be paid up by the BCCI–IPL for losses caused to the franchise. In an interesting twist, the franchise, instead of accepting the award, expressed its desire to be reinstated, and to participate in the next season of the IPL. It was unclear what the motive behind this stance was. The matter was said to be considered by the BCCI–IPL, and given the issues faced by the IPL just in putting together eight franchises for the ninth edition of the IPL, it may have been a win-win situation for both if Kochi had been reinstated. As it turned out, it wasn't, and the two interim franchises were awarded to Pune and Rajkot on 8 December 2015. It perhaps may not have been that simple to reinstate Kochi given the extent of controversy that the franchise had been in, leading to its original termination. The outcome of the arbitration may also have enthused other franchises and league partners who felt wronged by the BCCI to contemplate legal action in the future.

After the Kochi controversy, the other most public and bitter spat was between the Sahara Group and the BCCI–IPL over the treatment of the former's team, Pune Warriors. The Sahara Group, despite being the official sponsor of the national squad, never had a good run in the IPL. It entered the fray at a time when the league was settling in. The IPL's scheduling was at the mercy of the ICC granting it a window in future tours programmes, which it didn't do.[7] Therefore, despite expanding by 25 per cent, the number of days and matches of the tourney didn't increase in sync. This was the major bone of contention—the Pune ownership had made its business plan based on the playing of eighteen matches per season, when in actuality, the number of matches it played in each season that it was part of the IPL was never more than sixteen. The Pune ownership sought a reduction of the franchise fee, which anyone would have told them was not only an unenforceable request given the one-sided nature of the franchisee agreement, but also was never going to happen, given that it would have led to a mass demand of reduction by each franchise. Realizing that they had overpaid for the franchise, the Sahara Group had two additional grouses. Firstly, they felt that there was a dearth of players available to them, and they requested for more players to strengthen their squad. The request was refused, and Sahara asked the governing council to do away with the retention policy for players, and instead, put every player in the auction to ensure a level-playing field in terms of player acquisition for the franchises. Unsurprisingly and perhaps unfairly, this too was declined. The Warriors' performances were among the worst in each of the three seasons it played in the IPL. It finished last, second to last and last respectively. To add insult to injury, the Maharashtra Cricket Association had a dispute with Sahara regarding the naming rights of the Pune stadium, and even after it was resolved, Warriors were barred from playing at their home stadium because they allegedly had not met their payment obligations. In May 2013, the Sahara Group said it had had enough. It announced that it was withdrawing from the league, a follow-up to its original threat of withdrawal in 2012. It refused to make the franchise payment for the year, and also announced that effective from December 2013, it was backing out of the sponsorship of the Indian team as well. The announcement came just a few days after the spot-fixing scandal had broken, and the BCCI–IPL was in disaster-management mode. It took a hard stand just as it had done with the Kochi ownership. It cashed the bank guarantee and put Warriors on notice. But Sahara wasn't going to budge this time, and in October 2013, the BCCI terminated Pune Warriors, and the IPL was once again an eight-team league.

There shouldn't be an iron curtain when it comes to information on team and league ownership in professional sports leagues. The IPL is one of the only global sports leagues about which so little is known when it comes to the stakeholders. Until now, this was not really an issue; but transparency in ownership is a must, as is accountability of the league and confidence in its conforming to legal and ethical considerations. At the time the Kochi franchise was terminated and Modi was sent packing, the IPL should have taken some time to introspect and perhaps observe how other sports leagues had developed and coped over the last century. It didn't. By the time the Pune franchise was terminated, the BCCI should have realized that the IPL was in trouble, and then done some analysis and put into place measures to make the league more viable and sustainable. Again, it didn't but if it had, it would have been on stronger footing.

Historically, most other sports leagues had followed a more traditional path, with a gestation period of over fifty years for the most part before they became profitable—through organic growth, the merging of rival leagues over time, or even by breaking away and forming rebel leagues. Unlike the IPL, their growth was measured rather than exponential, and they gradually evolved into the global powerhouses that they are today. Over time, they also developed strong and effective systems that covered their regulatory, compliance, ethics, disciplinary, management and ownership issues with respect to league-mandated norms, something the IPL couldn't. In Chapter 6, we'll look at how the IPL is not a sports league in the true sense; from the perspective of sound processes, good governance and diligence, the BCCI–IPL has no valid excuse not to incorporate international best practices. It cost the IPL credibility and immediately arrested its growth circa 2013.

In 2013, to protect the interests of its franchises and restore team-owner confidence, the BCCI–IPL should have put in place a de facto office of the commissioner as is the case in each of the North American leagues. The office is the omnipotent lawmaker, and the commissioners, although usually elected by the owners or representatives/ stakeholders, wield significant clout and act as the enforcers and regulators. They are synonymous with their respective leagues, lending credibility, consistency and a long-term strategy/vision that enables accountability and promotes trust. They also have succession plans. Given the politics of the BCCI, and the power struggles within the BCCI–IPL, a succession plan or even the thought of one is laughable. And, of course, there wasn't any. With each new regime came a witch-hunt and marginal change. In large part, this is why the Supreme Court has now stepped in and insisted on change. It's still not too late. An external commissioner, as I have mentioned in different chapters of this book, may be the only way the league can survive; it will also help protect the viability and flexibility of the IPL's most valuable partners—the franchises. Given how the league is shaping up currently, the franchises may be the only partners willing to forgive and forget the league's missteps and inconsistency.

Originally, each of the franchises had stated plans to create independent entities that would go public through initial public offerings. That hasn't happened. In today's buyer's market, any franchise would be fortunate to even recover its original investment in the league. The league's most successful team and now its biggest pariah has had an interesting run in the area of valuations just this past year.

One of the most bizarre developments of 2015, a year in which there were plenty, was the rumoured logic-defying demerger of the CSK to a subsidiary of India Cements, at a valuation of INR 5 lakh.[8] It was yet another controversy for the CSK and Srinivasan, and this time it was in relation to the valuation its erstwhile parent company, India Cements Ltd, ascribed to it when selling it to a subsidiary. There was outrage within the new governing council and the Srinivasan-less board.

The outrage over the paltry valuation was justified, but it ignored the bigger concern in recent years. Franchises in the IPL are usually evaluated based on speculation, assumptions and hypotheticals, as opposed to tangible assets that a franchise possesses. An IPL franchise obtains value from intangible assets, value that is created due to the artificially imposed barrier to entry with respect to ownership of the right to participate in the IPL as a team. The value is consequently created through commercial rights, intellectual property rights, and the fact that there are limited number of rights that are granted to team owners, and this limited inventory of rights creates value for teams. Accordingly, the associated verticals are merchandising, central and team sponsorship/endorsement arrangements, marketing activations, gate receipts, and parallel promotional initiatives.

The glaring problem for team owners in the IPL when compared to other international leagues was, of course, that there were no tangible assets that they owned, such as real estate (stadiums), dependable and steady revenue from fans purchasing season tickets or even the right to leverage the commercial or virtual rights beyond the IPL and the CLT20 (Champions League). Even the rights that the teams exercise in the IPL are finite, mostly non-exclusive, and in favour of the board except during the IPL/CL season, and even then these are quite restricted.

The real impact would have been felt if the league had expanded along the planned lines, but that too has been unsuccessful—the new teams from Kochi and Pune withdrew or were terminated, and the Sun Group bought the terminated Deccan Chargers. The static number of franchises stalled a shrinking of central revenues in terms of percentage, but it hurt the franchises in the long run since the number of matches played remained the same. A shorter schedule also hampers brand-building initiatives that eventually lead to solid revenue streams, such as merchandising and team/city loyalty, the latter already affected by the relocation of matches due to BCCI's disputes with state cricket federations.

From a business perspective however, there are even bigger worries. The CSK franchise was bought in 2008 for US$91 million. It is undisputedly the most successful and consistent franchise, controversies aside. The most recent valuations done by international third parties of the franchise are hovering between approximately US$65 million to US$98 million. In real terms, taking into account inflation and purchasing-power parity across sports properties, the most successful franchise in the IPL is actually valued at less than its original purchase price.[9] This is assuming, of course, that there are actually interested potential buyers who are willing to take on the risk of liability and uncertainty of the acquired team's viability and sustainability in an extremely unstable environment. Between the liability and the risk of it being unviable, the purchase-price valuation of any team in the IPL is likely to further decrease, making the current franchise valuations less than their original auction-purchase prices, not only in real terms, but also in unadjusted terms. The CSK's valuation has led to action on the part of the board, because even by conservative estimates, this was an infinitesimal fraction of the already low estimates ascribed to the franchise by independent entities. That this was approved by the governing council of the time is extremely surprising; and the BCCI's working committee at its meeting on 26 April 2015 absolved the erstwhile governing council of any ill intentions on their part for the 'legal complexity' of the matter. It's almost certain that this will be scrutinized sooner rather than later. The BCCI refused to ratify the demerger of the CSK at that valuation, and legal options are still being explored. Meanwhile, Srinivasan is said to have transferred his shares of the CSK to a trust benefiting past players of the CSK. It was a confusing construct set up in all likelihood to show that he had no interest in the IPL franchise and so wouldn't come under the scanner of conflict of interest.

The confusion only intensified when India Cements transferred its CSK franchise rights to Chennai Super Kings Cricket Limited, a wholly owned subsidary during the financial year that concluded on 31 March 2015. For this to be approved, the BCCI required a comfort/guarantee letter from India Cements to ensure compliance with the obligations and responsibilities under the franchise agreement, and also required a tripartite novation agreement with the two entities and the board itself for assigning the rights and obligations to the new entity by India Cements. Shortly thereafter, it appears that the board of directors of the new entity, Chennai Super Kings Cricket Limited, approved the sale of the entire shareholding—an aggregate of 50,000 equity shares of INR 10 each, amounting to INR 5 lakh—to a trust called the India Cements Shareholder Trust. It appears that the overlap with India Cements continued because three of the independent directors of the new company were also trustees of the new trust, which had been established for the purpose of distribution of those shares to all non-promoter shareholders of India Cements. Interestingly, the shares that would have accrued to the promoters were to be allotted to another trust established for the benefit of ex-cricketers of the CSK. Such was the keenness of Srinivasan to make a triumphant return to the BCCI. Why he covets this post this much is still unknown, but what is certain is that he does, even at the cost of dissociating himself from his franchise, and maybe even from India Cements and family.

Now there is a real chance of the two transfers of the CSK's ownership not passing the smell test. Given the current scrutiny and the indication that the BCCI will reassess many of the transactions that may not appear entirely above board, there is a possibility that the initial sale may be questioned due to the extremely low valuation. Also, there will be questions regarding who the three independent directors are, since they have a common connection with the franchise. The second degree of separation is also going to be a question mark, since there is very little information available on its structure. An initial look at how it has been structured indicates that it has been done in a way that separates the ownership of the team from the original owners/promoters. This may not be enough to show a clean break from the original owners. The question of valuation, of course, would point at a financial loss to the BCCI more than the CSK because 5 per cent of five lakh rupees for a franchise once rumoured to be worth more than US$200 million was a rhetorical slap on many people's faces.

There will also be many questions raised by the current officials of the BCCI as to how the valuation was arrived at and approved. The second level of scrutiny might in the not-so-distant future be by the Justice Lodha Committee or officers appointed as per its recommendation by the board—namely the ombudsman or the ethics officer. So expect this to be scrutinized and quite likely revoked. The probable reason why it hasn't been delved into further is that the survival of the CSK franchise itself remains uncertain or at least suspended. To put the valuation of the CSK into perspective, it has to be noted that this wasn't a floundering franchise like the Deccan Chargers, which was essentially terminated, repackaged and then sold to the Sun Group at a valuation of approximately US$160 million. The CSK are the New England Patriots of the IPL if anything, and with a big brand captaining a successful side. The valuation doesn't reflect the brand the CSK has built, so there are obviously concerns about its credibility.

This leads to the way the BCCI now needs to handle the existing situation of change in control and/or ownership. It would also be a good time to look around at the leading sports leagues across the world, and try to draw parallels and related solutions. Even though there was hardly any due diligence done for determining the viability of potential owners, this can still be fixed. Even today, the BCCI–IPL can put in place prerequisites for ownership, and mandate that franchises fulfil obligations and meet the criteria. Independent of the franchise agreements being signed, these changes can be made in the IPL rules and regulations in light of the Supreme Court's view. There should have been a clear-cut methodology in place that governed how the IPL did its due diligence when inducting new ownership.

Globally, there isn't a hard and fast rule that describes the structure of professional sports leagues; nor is there any such rule when it comes to the ownership pattern of the teams within them. Yes, it is true that ownership in professional sports leagues—especially where there are large consortiums owning a particular team—is hard to regulate and verify. However, the first step is transparency, and a clear-cut guideline of ownership which would stipulate the ownership eligibility criterion. Once the eligibility criterion is met, one can verify the funding and ownership. The NFL and EPL are two of the most profitable and popular sports leagues in the world. Their respective league rules however mandate contrasting ownership structures.

The NFL, arguably the most lucrative and successful professional sports league in the world, has a somewhat unique ownership structure, one which allows it to maintain strict control over management and ownership of teams. Unlike other leagues, there is absolutely no corporate ownership allowed, and the ownership groups must contain twenty-four or fewer individuals. The general partner and his/her family must together own 30 per cent or more of the team, and any change in ownership is strictly regulated. The reasoning behind this is also linked to ensuring focused management with a singular vision as well as consistent and long-term ownership. The ownership, for the most part, is transparent and, for all intents and purposes, above board.

The EPL is the exact opposite, where size and influence have mattered. The sale or purchase of Manchester United, Chelsea, Liverpool and Arsenal are frequently debated, and due diligence and background checks that have been conducted are sometimes questioned with respect to their thoroughness. The ownership guidelines have been questioned too, along with their implementation.

The EPL too faces questions about the nature of foreign investment in its clubs. While foreign investment has propped up the league and made it a global powerhouse, many of the clubs are debt-ridden, and the cleanliness of the funds and ownership has been a subject of mass speculation.

Other professional sports leagues follow different patterns. Some leagues own their teams outright; investors then pay for the rights to manage and host a particular team's games. There is no clear-cut formula for how leagues are owned globally.

While foreign ownership in the US leagues hasn't been much of a factor, the EPL, on the other hand, has seen a mass influx of foreign investment, and there are concerns as to whether or not the ownership guidelines would need to be tweaked. The Thaksin fiasco with Manchester City—in which the controversial former prime minister of Thailand briefly became the storied club's majority shareholder before selling it out to an Abu Dhabi–based consortium—led to calls for curbing foreign investment. But what the debt-ridden EPL clubs desperately need is equity financing so that the EPL cannot put a blanket ban or too strict a limitation on foreign funding.

Instead, a more rigorous 'know your investor' credential and background check is likely so as to ensure the sanctity of management and ownership of these teams. This is also something the IPL can adopt in order to avoid future spats, and ensure that there is a systematic procedure in place. If it learns from the EPL, it has found a good model to emulate.[10]

Designations that are misleading or roles that are not defined, as well as gaps in public monikers versus available bandwidth for addressing governance and integrity lapses are additional challenges that the IPL faces. In part due to the need for importance, and largely because the league came before its systems, designations have caused a lot of grief for many of those connected to the league. While the dichotomy between the IPL and an international professional sports league will be highlighted in Chapter 6, for the present analysis it would be important to know how designations and role ambiguity have hurt the functioning of the IPL.

As with everything else the IPL associated itself with, it fell prey to what it felt were the dominant attributes of Indian society and culture. Egos frequently rule culture and society, and in the IPL it extended to positions, designations and titles. Most professionals in India use designations that extoll their positions, and the name associated with certain positions or profiles matters more than an accurate depiction of the role one actually performs at a structure. At times harmless, however at other times designations and definitions take on a more material role with serious implications. In India, testosterone too plays a bigger part than we would like to admit. Some titles or designations are driven by our cultural and societal wants and aspirations—the lure of ownership and being considered 'bosses' obviously trumps mundane middle-management designations, which while uninspiring, are a more accurate reflection of the role that we sometimes perform.

The IPL was no different, and designations played a huge part in building the image of the 'league', from its inception right up to the spot-fixing scandal. When the foundation of a sector is based on a fluid structure, it's imperative that the powers that be put thought into what the future persona of their corporate entity will be. In the IPL, there were two categories of corporate identities—those who leveraged it for brand and fame, and those who did all they could to hide behind layers of corporate trickery so as to avoid the public eye.

In the IPL, bigger was substantially better, and the western world's professional sports monikers raced downstream towards their places of honour in Indian sports culture and lore. It started with the adoption of titles that didn't actually reflect the activity or purpose for which they were adopted. In 2008, we had a forty-five-day cricket tournament generously laced with a carnival environment being called a 'league', and at its helm we had a 'commissioner'.

Now, real leagues across the world are structured differently than mere tournaments, taking into account governance and compliance platforms that give them the authority and autonomy to function as independent entities, exempt from government intervention except when falling afoul of law in clearly defined circumstances such as fraud, embezzlement, aggravated torts, perjury, and sometimes, anti-trust. Similarly, 'franchises' or 'teams' too have a far more rigorous compliance list than merely choosing players, cheerleaders and sponsors. The 'commissioner' runs the entire show, and also makes far-reaching decisions by involving a group of advisors, team owners, player representatives and government authorities. The commissioner has broad powers, but more than that, binding obligations and responsibilities. The buck literally stops with the commissioner, and we have two recent examples of how a commissioner can rise or fall in the public eye through his actions and obligations.

In the NBA and the NFL, in the past two years alone there have been two major controversies pertaining to a team in each league. The NBA's Los Angeles Clippers were caught in a racism-related scandal when the owner at the time, Donald Sterling, was accused of making racist statements about African Americans. The players and coach threatened to boycott the team, and the league stood behind them. The league's new commissioner, Adam Silver, expelled Sterling from the NBA, and forced him to sell the team. The team was sold for a significant premium over its valuation, for nearly US$2 billion by former Microsoft CEO Steve Ballmer. The premium aside, the decision was an exclamation point for the league when it showed in a single move that it was the authoritative body and that it had a zero-tolerance policy for any action that would bring disrepute to the NBA.

The NFL is also in the middle of a groundbreaking tiff with its premier team, New England Patriots, over a scandal known as 'deflate-gate'. The controversy revolves around certain actions that the Patriots and their star quarterback, Tom Brady, took during home games in Massachusetts regarding the inflation level of the balls used. An investigation showed that the inflation levels were significantly lower than the allowed levels, and the NFL, through its commissioner Roger Goodell after a brief hearing, suspended and fined Brady and the Patriots. The matter was then taken to court, where it is still being argued. This was a controversial move given the profile of the individuals concerned, but frequently it is the commissioner who must take a stance, rigid or flexible, against franchises that they feel are not living up to the league's values or expectations. The BCCI too needs to take strong decisions if the IPL is to restore its credibility.

One of the biggest causes of confusion and eventually governance failure is the obsession that the IPL has with designations. We all know how designations panned out in the IPL when it came to meeting obligations and responsibilities. The commissioner was unceremoniously dumped and his supporters, except those who changed allegiances, were extricated from the inner core and left out in the cold. For a commissioner with limited obligations and responsibilities, a coup to ensure his departure was really not that difficult to manoeuvre. Modi, of course, has continued his crusade from abroad but the challenges of an actual return to Indian cricket appear to be significant, even for him. When it came to designations however, Modi's folly was overshadowed by a far greater imprudence— one which caused Modi's successor to abdicate and face opposition unlike any of his predecessors. It all started with a relatively harmless move by Srinivasan's son-in-law Meiyappan. Tasked with being the face of the CSK, Meiyappan proudly donned the designation of 'team principal'. In the IPL, such things were commonplace. Each individual outdid the other in finding ways to beat their own chests and declare ownership. Especially those who had little or no ownership of the franchises in the first place. Meiyappan, by all accounts, was holding place on behalf of his extremely powerful father-in-law, who at the time couldn't openly manage the team, despite his very controversial move of convincing the BCCI to allow cricket officials to own commercial interests in cricket—in this case, a team in the IPL. The infamous Clause 6.2.4 of the BCCI's Rules and Regulations is discussed in detail in Chapter 4, but for our purpose right now, it is enough to know that conflict of interest concerns were wiped out by the modification to the obligations governing the roles of cricket officials and owners of commercial interests. So in came India Cements as team owners, and in came Meiyappan as team principal.

Now, a misleading designation could be harmful for all concerned—team owner, the league, the individual, and any person or entity who reasonably believed that Meiyappan actually was what his designation/title depicted.

Sometimes a name or title creates such negativity that one wonders why it ever came into use. The very fact that the BCCI is for the 'control' of cricket in India instead of the global norm of 'committee', 'association' or even 'council'—like ICC—makes one wonder why it was necessary to name it thus. Dichotomous designations occur frequently in most sports federations in India.

Perhaps in the not-so-distant past, not enough attention was given to titles and designations, but this argument won't hold water, going forward. A 'team principal' will probably mean a team owner—one who has access to privileged information and owes a binding responsibility to the league, to shareholders, and to all employees (where applicable). Going forward, having a designation that implies a leadership position without the requisite responsibilities and obligations should possibly end up as an actionable offence if addressed properly in the national and state sports fraud laws in India.

The Justice Lodha Committee has had a large part to play in disciplining the IPL. The committee posed some serious obstacles to the future of the IPL. Empowered by the court to delve into the nature of governance and into integrity breaches within the IPL, it found malfeasance in its first report not just at the level of the individuals under scrutiny—Meiyappan and Kundra—but also found the two franchises to be at fault, suspending them for two years. The faults stemmed from breaches of the IPL Operational Rules, the IPL Regulations, the IPL Anti-Corruption Code, the IPL Code of Conduct for Players and Match Officials, and critically, the franchise agreements.

The franchises, through their key personnel, committed acts that brought both the game and the league into disrepute. A representation to that effect by the committee was telling on the franchise's ability to retain its ownership of the team. The agreements signed by all the franchises were extremely one-sided in favour of the BCCI. Since it was a 'take it or leave it' opportunity at that time, no modifications were probably made to any franchise agreement. With both the court and the committee concluding that unethical activities took place, the franchises ought to have been terminated. The board clearly had the ability to terminate both franchises with immediate effect in accordance with Clause 11.3 (c) of the agreement on breach of contract. The clause states:

> BCCI–IPL may terminate this Agreement with immediate effect by written notice if: the Franchise, any Franchisee Group Company and/or any owner acts in any way which has a material adverse effect upon the reputation or standing of the League, BCCI–IPL, the Franchisee, the Team (or any other team in the League) and/or the game of cricket.

This could have been interpreted broadly by the BCCI in its favour. Not only that, a clear breach of contract occurred when a team official, and not the franchise as a whole, committed an act that went against the tenets of proper conduct as stipulated in the IPL regulations and code of conduct. Vicarious liability principles too would extend to every aspect of the current scenario. There are strict obligations imposed on the franchises—the most relevant of which is the operational obligation where the franchise represents and warrants that it 'shall procure that all players and Team officials and/or employees and any other person acting for or on behalf of the Franchisee and/or the Team comply with the Regulations during each Season and that the Team complies with the Laws of Cricket during any Matches'.[11] Even the most optimistic and proactive member of either of the two franchises would have found it difficult to see a silver lining mitigating the obvious breaches of contract. Further, multiple breaches of the IPL regulations had already been noted by the Justice Mudgal Committee, the Justice Lodha Committee and the court (discussed in Chapter 4).

There is, of course, little doubt that Meiyappan's and Kundra's actions or omissions have brought the game into disrepute; it has had an adverse effect on the franchises, the league and the BCCI. The interpretation of disrepute in terms of sports contracts is usually broad enough to include the committing of any illegal activity, and in India betting is illegal. And that is just one example. Also, given how unfavourably the court viewed the BCCI and the IPL, a termination would conceivably have been supported and in fact encouraged by the court and its appointed committees. In its observations, the court implied as much.[12] In fact, Justice Lodha mentioned in an interview how only the BCCI–IPL could terminate the franchises as per the agreement—a contractual arrangement that the court and the committees were clearly loath to interfere with.[13]

From the court's perspective, the maximum possible intervention it could make under the BCCI–IPL's regulations was sanctioning and suspension of the individuals and franchises, something which it has already ordered. Rather than act as a commercial arbitrator on individual business decisions, it is far more likely that the court, through its committees, may recommend the suspension of the league altogether, in the interest of preserving and perpetuating the sanctity of cricket. It would be an extreme step, but if as in the past, the BCCI doesn't act proactively and authoritatively this time, the suspension of the IPL could well be the eventual outcome.

The IPL crew is a worried lot these days. They have had a really bad time in arbitration and litigation, and not just due to the PILs. The Kochi arbitration and the reversals of the RR and KXIP terminations have jarred the board. It has valid concerns. The commercial risks are, of course, significant for the BCCI, and that is why it has dragged its feet on this. There is a very real risk of the value of the existing franchises plummeting. This would, in turn, see the bid prices for new franchises drop to levels even lower than when the league first started. It wouldn't be a shock if the going price for a new franchise is in the range of US$40–60 million.

The immediate termination of the CSK and the RR franchises should stand the legal test. More importantly, it will convey to the court that the BCCI–IPL is willing to change, and at the same time rid the current regime of the stigma attached to the CSK. The two existing franchises ought to have been retired, and their intangible goodwill (if any remains) be assigned to two new franchises that don't carry the liabilities and baggage of the previous ownerships. There are no assets that exist except for the intellectual property of the teams; therefore it will be prudent to dissolve the two teams and allocate the players to the new franchises, with an option for them to accept or decline. If ever the BCCI wanted to send a strong signal that it was righting the course and was intent on bringing strict accountability to its commercial entities, this would be it. It would be important however to ensure that both the franchises are treated equally and not subjectively. On 18 October 2015, the board took the safe route and decided not to terminate the CSK and the RR. This decision, taken in the first meeting presided over by Shashank Manohar in his second term as BCCI president, was a disappointing and disjointed one. For the ninth season, the board mandated an eight-team format, with bids being accepted for franchises interested in owning and operating teams for the two seasons when the CSK and the RR stand suspended. Until the AGM (annual general meeting), it was unclear if the new franchises would just be bridge entities with a finite two-year window until 2018, following which the CSK and the RR would return. Prior to the AGM, on 31 October there were a few hints on the set-up, presumably after these were discussed with the remaining franchises.

In yet another innovative allocation methodology devised by the BCCI, it appeared that the bridge entities would have a temporary right to run a team for two years. In what was termed a 'reverse bidding' process, the interested bidders could bid either a positive amount or a negative amount for the rights. A positive amount would mean that if a successful franchise bid INR5 crore, for example, that was the amount the BCCI would pay the franchise as compensation for the operating costs. If a successful bidder had bid a negative amount, say INR (–) 5 crore, it meant the bidder would pay BCCI INR5 crore for the right to operate the franchises. The reasoning behind this was that the temporary franchises would not receive any revenue from the central revenue pool, only from the local revenue pool. So to offset the costs, the BCCI was willing to subsidize the successful bidders if need be. The franchises were also to be given the right to choose any city from which to operate their franchises, so as to generate local support, and a separate player auction or draft would first be held for the temporary franchises presumably with players from the suspended franchises in the player pool, before a separate auction for the remaining franchises.

As it turned out, the board's concerns were unjustified. Not only was there plenty of interest in acquiring an interim franchise by established corporates, the formula used was so successful that the board not only saved money, but is expected to earn nearly INR170 crore annually from the two-year deal. In all, twenty-one potential franchises are said to have bought the bid submission documents,[14] while five entities actually ended up bidding. On 8 December 2015, Pune was awarded to Sanjiv Goenka's New Rising for a fee of INR 16 crore, and the Intex Group was awarded the Rajkot franchise for INR10 crore. The reverse bidding worked to a charm in that not only did the two new interim franchises agree to forgo any portion of the central sponsorship revenues (estimated to be approximately INR75 crore per franchise), they instead agreed to pay the board the winning amount for the right to operate teams.[15] It's a strong message for the BCCI's detractors. Although there were fewer bidders than one would have expected overall, the fact remains that there were entities willing to forgo central revenue and actually put in their own money— almost to the tune of INR100–120 crore annually—just to be a part of the action in the IPL. That is impressive, and should restore confidence to the franchises of what their brand will be worth going forward. After all, the kind of investment envisioned is for a short-term association that will yield no preference or long-term benefits from the BCCI to the interim franchises.[16]

Based on the limited information available, it appears that the interim franchises will not have the right of first refusal or the right of first offer to own a permanent franchise if and when the BCCI–IPL does decide to expand the league. It appeared as though the board was keen to show a meritorious due process to those members now out of power. The official reason for not terminating the two franchises was that the Justice Lodha Committee had ordered merely a suspension of two years, so it was beyond the scope of the governing council and the board to recommend a punishment above and beyond that. What this ignores is that the court and its committees are still loath to interfering in the inner workings and contractual understandings that the board and the IPL have got into. Justice Lodha said as much in an interview following the order. So to hide behind the Justice Lodha Committee's order could backfire for the board over time. This could be another opportunity lost for the board at a time when it needed to throw caution to the winds.

With the IPL's affinity with termination and withdrawals, one would predict that ten teams is not a sustainable number. But let's assume for the sake of argument that ten teams are fielded in IPL's eleventh season. Besides the logistical complexity and the absence of a clear window in which to host nearly eighty days' worth of matches, the revenue potential and dilution will need to be very closely looked at. It's going to be a crowded set with revenues being fought over in a structure that has at no point until now seemed capable of putting together a league that has any more than eight teams at best. The CSK and the RR will be trying to stitch together a return to the event, and try to pick up from where they had left. Whether or not they get their players back or not is another big question mark. And what if the two temporary franchises end up being a success and exemplary models of governance and on-field performance? Will it really be a prudent move to end their run with the league and bring back the two franchises that had caused all the heartache for the board? These are all questions that won't be answered until 2018, by when many more things would have changed with the IPL.

Today the IPL continues to make news. As recently as in September 2015, Lalit Modi found himself in the middle of yet another controversy. For years it was whispered loudly that Modi had interests in certain franchises of the IPL. With most things IPL, it was always more of a rumour, and since the ownership patterns were so intricately confusing, very little had been traced back to Modi over the years, despite the best efforts of his detractors. Now however, it came to light through leaked emails that Modi may well have ownership stakes in three of the original eight franchises. Nothing has yet been confirmed, but this may just be the window of opportunity the BCCI has been looking for, and expect it to explore this in great detail. This may also lend credibility to the Kochi franchise's stance and the assertions made that Modi was keen to scuttle the Kochi bid since he was interested more in an Ahmedabad franchise, and had allegedly supported the Adani Group's bid for one of the franchises. This, of course, has only been rumoured and never proven, but for those who have felt that Modi had a lot more skin in the game than just as the chief administrator of the league, this may be the Pandora's box they had all been waiting for to open.[17] To be fair, since the initial buzz of speculation this rumour has somewhat died down, but each day is one new opportunity in the IPL when it comes to owning a scandal or success.[18]

What's interesting in today's environment is that contracts with the BCCI–IPL, no matter how one-sided they were in favour of the board, have usually not held up in court. The many travails of broadcast partners were discussed in Chapter 1, and some of the franchises too have gone to court or for arbitration and frequently emerged victorious. It means that the courts are willing to override onerous contractual arrangements if they feel parity is missing. Also, it shows that the BCCI is unable to stifle its business partners or even coerce them. This level playing field has changed the balance of power, and could mean a louder clamour for rights from the franchises. In the current environment, neither the board nor the league can afford negative publicity.

Owning a franchise in today's IPL is a risky proposition as there are hardly any buyers out there. Most have held back plans until there is clarity on the league going forward. Guilty by association, franchises can be liable for a lot more than just the franchise fee, so being an owner carries a lot more responsibility than just putting together a playing eleven and turning up to cheer for the team. The lightning quick progress to a leading sports league has been halted at least temporarily and many of the franchises have faced far too many controversies and inconsistent treatment during their tenure. It is a far cry from how franchises are treated in other sports leagues, where owners of teams have the authority to make important and fiduciary decisions, including whom to appoint as the CEO or commissioner. It's quite a contrast to the IPL's governing council, even in its new form as envisioned by Manohar. Unless the communication between the league and the teams increases and the involvement in decision-making for the league by the franchises increases, voluntary franchise owners will become a rare breed. For now, speculation has been taken out of the equation, and one way or the other the franchises will have a somewhat clearer picture of the team owners' landscape. A critical phase for team ownership lies ahead when the true tests of self-sufficiency begin.

4

Conflict of Interest

Conflict of interest has become the single most relevant term that is synonymous with Indian cricket in 2016. The conflict of interest phenomenon has shaped how ethics in cricket is to be determined. A working definition for conflict of interest is 'a situation that has the potential to undermine the impartiality of a person because of the possibility of a clash between the person's self-interest and professional interest or public interest'. If that isn't a familiar theme for Indian cricket, one wonders what possibly is.

In an extremely short span of just a few months, two of India's iconic cricketers, a current BCCI official, and other former players have already been faced with conflict of interest hearings in front of the ombudsman, Justice A.P. Shah. Sourav Ganguly was involved in a PIL by a gentleman who questioned Ganguly's conflict of interest with regard to the bidding process for the interim franchises. Ganguly is a minority stakeholder in the Indian Super League (ISL) club Atlético de Kolkata whose majority partner is Sanjiv Goenka's New Rising, which successfully bid for the Pune IPL franchise. Ganguly's place in the IPL governing council and his failure to recuse himself from the process was questioned, but given the nature of how the process unfolded, and also the fact that he had virtually no role to play in the choosing of the successful franchises, the ombudsman didn't feel there was any conflict. The decision does appear to be the right one, but given that Ganguly's role in the governing council will include sitting in on matters that involve franchises, including the Pune franchise, this issue may come up soon again. The second conflict of interest matter had a different verdict altogether and related to whether or not there was a conflict for Harbhajan Singh with regard to the clothing brand Bhajji Sports that provides apparel to six Ranji teams, although Singh has stated that his mother owns the company, not he. Justice Shah disagreed and directed Singh to relinquish his role in the company and provide a clear undertaking to the board to eliminate any conflict of interest.

Justice Shah has been categorically addressing potential conflicts, pressing upon those involved with cricket that they must declare their conflicts, and/or take appropriate action to eliminate the conflict.[1] This at the very least is heartening, and a positive move, even if hastened by the Supreme Court's directives.

Nothing has caused more grief to the BCCI–IPL than the conflict of interest controversy. Although conflicts had existed in the system for decades, the controversy was unearthed only recently. It was the most devastating because unlike an integrity lapse or scrutiny oversight such as spot-fixing, conflict of interest hit at the nucleus of the board's activities and dealings. It brought the board to the courts and allowed the judiciary to regulate cricket administration.

Conflict of interest is broad enough to cover any action or relationship which can potentially compromise decision-making, or unjustly enrich an individual or an entity. For the BCCI–IPL, the clause that broke through the shell of inner workings is the iconic Clause 6.2.4 of the BCCI regulations. The clause in its controversial avatar read as follows: 'No administrator shall have directly or indirectly any commercial interest in any of the events of BCCI, excluding IPL and CLT20.'

It was this revised clause which allowed Srinivasan to own a team in the IPL and it is this clause, which if retained in its original version would have prevented much of what went wrong with the BCCI–IPL in the context of conflict of interest; at least since we now have reason to believe that conflict of interest was pervasive in the BCCI, and manifested in the IPL.[2] The original and unaltered version of the clause read as follows: 'No administrator shall have, directly or indirectly, any commercial interest in the matches and events conducted by the board.'

This clause did not solve the basic problem of preventing conflicts of interest for non-administrators, but kept actionable a breach of this basic conflict of interest. Functioning as a private body, the board had very little accountability in the years leading up to the IPL's launch, and for at least a few seasons of the league. Yes, eyebrows were raised periodically at the CSK, and the board's profitability remained a topic revolving around unjust enrichment; But until the spot-fixing scandal erupted, no one really had an inkling of how conflict of interest would trigger the IPL's overhaul.

It was unearthed when the Justice Mudgal Committee was tasked with determining corruption and spot-fixing in the IPL. Then the Supreme Court intervened through the course of the hearings on the spot-fixing scandal. It has now stretched across the various verticals, and today the board is on the defensive. Let's be objective—conflict of interest is almost unavoidable within the parameters of a particular ecosystem. And not all conflict of interest is harmful, if it is tackled effectively. Srinivasan could actually make a case for being transparent in that he was working within the legal parameters of having a commercial interest in the IPL, under the revision of the clause that had been allowed when he wasn't yet president of the board. From his perspective, he and India Cements played by the rules, at least in terms of ownership and transparency. It was however his reaction to the spot-fixing scandal and his position of prominence impacting the BCCI's response to many of the steps that were deemed necessary, that put him and the board in the difficult position it is in today.

Conflict of interest can be tackled effectively in a few ways, all of which are intuitive. Eliminating two counterproductive roles, that benefit the person who is on both sides of the table or benefits from one side of the table, is intuitive. Recusing oneself when one's commercial interest is being probed, and one's relative is being interrogated, ought to be an obvious step. Ensuring that individuals with fiduciary responsibilities should not use the information they receive confidentially for personal and illegal gain is elementary. But it turns bizarre when a national team selector is also an IPL team's brand ambassador, and when the said IPL team belongs to the board's president. In today's IPL, conflict of interest has marred four key grey areas. The first and most challenging is the conflict between cricket administrators and their commercial interests in cricket—facilitated, before it was struck down, by the revised clause 6.2.4. There are other ways around it still, which will be explained shortly.

The second and quite worrying is the conflict between active players owning shares or equity in sports management companies that represent them and other active players. This has the potential to directly or indirectly impact their selection choices of the playing eleven, and overall of the conflicted players' teammates' careers. The third is a combination of non-traditional versions of conflict of interest that appear to compromise positions of individuals involved with the BCCI and the IPL—we have examples of owners of franchises sharing information with outsiders for personal gain, manifesting in illegal betting or trading on inside information. It's no secret that Meiyappan and Kundra head this list. This was the basis of the spot-fixing controversy and the overlap with conflict of interest. There are other forms of conflict of interest in this category: former players employed by the BCCI–IPL who hold positions as television commentators, or who serve dual roles as team mentors or brand ambassadors of franchises while also serving in a capacity as team selectors or coaches for the BCCI. Sunil Gavaskar, Ravi Shastri, Anil Kumble, and Sourav Ganguly were mentioned even by the BCCI in its submission to the Court.[3] Since Shashank Manohar's presidency, many of these conflicts are being addressed and rectified. The fourth and most likely to be damaging to the reputation of the BCCI–IPL in future is the duality of roles performed by public officials who hold positions in the BCCI. I had earlier mentioned the Justice Lodha Committee's recommendation to exclude ministers and government officials from the board's administration. The current IPL chairman, Rajeev Shukla, is a politician. The secretary of the BCCI, Anurag Thakur, is a politician. A member of the present IPL governing council, Jyotiraditya Scindia, is a politician. Former BCCI president and the current nominee for the ICC, if Manohar is unavailable, Sharad Pawar, is a politician. Many of the state associations' presidents or board members are politicians. Quite a few of them have done good work, most recently Thakur. But the politician–cricket official dual role has caused concern to the judiciary, to the public at large, and to the reputation of cricket and the IPL. It has also been the cause of many of the conflict of interest controversies, adversely impacting the politicians as well as cricket's overall health.

It's true that individuals who are businessmen (read: Srinivasan or Modi) or professionals (read: Shashank Manohar in his first stint at the helm) have not always had a stellar run at administering cricket. That said, the first move that will probably need to be made by the BCCI or imposed on it by the Supreme Court would be the restrictions on involvement by active politicians in the IPL, and in future, the BCCI as a whole. For the IPL, the conflict of interest controversy took centre stage during the spot-fixing scandal, but the first great fiasco in the IPL happened much earlier than that. The franchise expansion auction of the IPL was both its biggest success and, soon after, its biggest failure. I have already detailed the Kochi franchise's story and its eventual collapse. The Kochi franchise was a primary example of conflict of interest, and an extremely warped set of events. There was a lot more to it than just the sweat-equity component. Sundar Raman for an extended period of time was on the hot seat for his alleged closeness to a bookie, and his influential role in the BCCI facilitated by Srinivasan. He was recruited by Modi when the IPL began in 2008. Even after Modi's suspension and eventual ban, Raman continued his service to the league. It was only once Shashank Manohar, who had in the past questioned Raman's continuing presence in the IPL, returned to head the BCCI that Raman resigned. The timing of the resignation was such that it happened prior to the Justice Lodha Committee's final order on the functioning of the BCCI and its officials, and it perhaps raised the eyebrows of those closely following this entire episode. Raman had thus far merely been questioned, although the questioning by the court was quite pointed. He needn't have worried. The Justice Lodha Committee, in its report, cleared Raman of any wrongdoing, and the Supreme Court accepted the recommendation. Interestingly, Manohar had earlier said this about Raman:

Raman should have gone immediately after the Mudgal Committee report found him prima facie guilty of wrongdoing. He ought to have stepped down immediately at that time. Now, to restore the faith of people in IPL and the game, Raman needs to go.[4]

In hindsight, Modi and Raman may not have had much in common despite being part of the founding team that brought the IPL together, but in one goal they seem to have stood united: to ensure that Kochi either became discouraged or was thwarted in its efforts to win a bid for an IPL franchise. Raman had an interesting role in Kochi's pre-auction due diligence. A few days before the bids for the two new franchises closed, an email went out from Raman to an employee of the IPL. The email contained revenue projections for potential franchises in the expansion auction. The employee forwarded the email to her father, whose personal assistant then forwarded the same email to a friend. The friend was said to be interested in helping an IPL team come to his adopted state, and the information would have been useful in his evaluations.[5] There are a few things wrong in the scenario, but nothing really outrageous. It was the identities of the individuals in this scenario that caused a huge controversy. Raman sent the email to a 'junior employee', whose name happened to be Poorna Patel. He claims that further transmission of the email was neither something that he was aware of nor something he had authorized. Poorna Patel, as it turns out, is the daughter of the then federal minister for civil aviation, Praful Patel. Patel's personal assistant forwarded the email to his friend, Shashi Tharoor, who was very actively pitching for the franchise to come to Kochi.[6] Now here's the rub—the information in the email, besides being extremely confidential, did not paint a rosy picture. According to the projections, neither of the franchises could reasonably expect to be profitable until the tenth year of their existence at the earliest. A net loss of more than INR600 crore was expected according to the projections.[7]

Anyone wanting to own the team ought to have been deterred, but the Kochi consortium went ahead anyway, and won the bid. Later, the projections were declared to be overly pessimistic, and the rumour spread as to how Raman had intentionally directed inaccurate projections to Tharoor via Patel, in an effort to deter the bid. The questions that arose were whether Patel, through his daughter Poorna, was receiving classified information on a potential bid he was looking to make. Patel said he had no such plans, and was merely doing his friend Tharoor a favour by giving the information. This was puzzling, because if the information wasn't classified, it needn't have been specially requested of the IPL's upper management. There were more questions than answers after this came into the public domain, and the high-profile nature of this was attributed to the political nature of the controversy.

The conflict of interest component was intrinsic but not proven, primarily because it became moot. Tharoor had to resign, and the issue remained one of sweat equity and eventually of the termination of the franchise. Patel and his daughter were dragged in on a different matter related to the misuse of scheduled Air India flights, when it was alleged that three scheduled flights had been taken out of service and used as private charter planes to ferry IPL players and officials.[8] These allegations were denied, including by Air India, and the matter eventually quietened down.[9] For the board it was fortunate that it did, because the embarrassment that this conflict of interest could have caused was significant. Patel's closeness to the BCCI–IPL had to do with the president of his political party who also happened to be one of the most powerful men in cricket—Sharad Pawar.

The conflict of interest regarding ownership began, of course, with the commencement of the league, and there were two kinds right off the bat. There were the allegations of indirect and absentee ownership by Modi, and there were those linked to the open ownership of a team by a powerful board member. At the time, the existing situation was accepted by everyone, at least until the Kochi issue erupted. Conflict of interest had more or less been a regrettable necessity of the BCCI–IPL, an accepted part of its nucleus and no efforts were made to form a Chinese wall or exclude dual roles. In all honesty, if not for the defining nature of the spot-fixing scandal in 2013, not much was likely to change in the BCCI's IPL. If anything, the nature of the CSK's inclusion in the IPL should have been ample proof of how personal interests trumped the greater good of the IPL.

Clause 6.2.4 being amended meant the duality of roles allowed for the divergence of priorities. One can't overstate the importance of the amendment, for it legalized a component that clearly would never have been allowed in the first place. So glaring is the adverse conflict of interest allowed by the amendment that even the court intervened to the extent that it struck it down as illegal and untenable. As the national sports federation for cricket, the BCCI has the sole responsibility of promoting and developing the sport of cricket. Improving infrastructure, providing top-calibre coaching, ensuring that regional, state and national tournaments were conducted throughout the year, and fielding the best possible squad for the national team—that is the entire extent of the responsibility of the BCCI. It's not about earning as much money as it possibly can; it's not about owning and operating an entity like the IPL solely for commercial gain; and above all else, it's not about enriching its officials through an inside track on commercial opportunities within cricket, including especially the ownership of a team in a league owned by the BCCI. The gravy train had to be derailed at some point, and that's what happened in 2015.

The conflict of interest between owners mingling freely with the team in the dugout and advising routinely on team matters was caused by the freewheeling, eager-to-please nature of the IPL. Conflict of interest in the IPL between owners and players occurred for a very simple reason: the eagerness of each party to please the other in a collegial environment. Where else in the world does one see owners of teams exchanging high-fives during a game with their star players? Or an intense discussion between the owner and his team captain and/or coach prior to and right after the toss? Or a nightly party where everyone mingled with everyone for reasons unknown, and where most likely the most damage was caused in terms of exchange of information? The IPL was just asking for trouble, and the trouble came in bunches. Meiyappan and Kundra bore the brunt of ownership miscues, but every franchise owner has been in closer proximity to his/her team players than is ideal for a league looking to curb the easy leaking of vital information.

Conflict of interest became a focal point of the judiciary's probe when during the course of its investigation into the spot-fixing scandal, the Justice Mudgal Committee's attention was directed towards the pervasive issues that conflict of interest was causing. The committee in its initial report observed certain aspects. It observed the issues prevalent in the revised clause 6.2.4 and recommended that the court take a closer look at it. Next, in the interest of the league, it recommended that the IPL be a stand-alone commercial entity with representatives from the franchises, BCCI and broadcasters, forming a part of the governing body, which would also include independent professional directors. It recommended that the BCCI adopt a system of registering player agents. Before registering player agents, it felt there should be an examination of the agents to confirm their understanding of the rules and regulations of the BCCI and the IPL. Besides this, the antecedents of the player agent should also be verified so that dubious elements with links to bookies or the underworld are not given registration as a player agent. Finally, it felt that players should not be allowed to own any stakes or interests in player agencies or companies involved with cricket unless such interests are in the nature of sponsorship or endorsements.

The conflict of interest which arises for former and current cricketers is a particularly tricky one. The BCCI–IPL being extremely closely knit, many former players are contracted to the IPL or one of its franchises. For the flagship Indian cricket league, everyone's involvement in some capacity or the other is expected. There are however two situations which can be either vulnerable to conflict or automatically lead to a harmful conflict of interest. For former players, a role as coach of the BCCI's national teams or/and as mentor, coach or advisor of an IPL team is not problematic. Nor is it problematic if former players take on commentator's positions during the national team's matches, and also act as advisors, mentors or coaches for franchises. The problem arises when a decision-making role within the BCCI's committees, such as that of a selector or a coach mingles with being a mentor, advisor or coach in the IPL. At that time, the individual concerned must choose one of the two roles. Or, even simpler is for the individual to retain the role, but recuse himself from selection decisions on players belonging to the IPL team which he is mentoring, coaching or advising.

The additional role that former players are now taking on is as owners or managers of player representation companies, often in partnership with active players who have decision-making roles in the national squad. This should be prohibited for a variety of reasons as this is a harmful conflict of interest in every which way. Active players should simply not be allowed to invest in, or own equity in commercial enterprises that represent other players; they should also not be in a position of power or prominence which would benefit other players contracted to their player management company. The IPL is where the most opportunities for active players getting entangled in conflicts of interest arise. It is at the IPL level therefore that players should undertake not to be part of any conflict of interest roles.

Active players should not be employed by any corporation or individual with equity in a team in the IPL when the players are contracted to the BCCI–IPL. Similarly, former players contracted to the BCCI should not be employed by or become consultants to any private sector entity with active interest in the BCCI–IPL. The same should hold for any personnel of any of the IPL teams, or of the central league itself. The only exception can be former players with no direct role with the BCCI being allowed to own or be employed by player representation companies, provided there is no conflict of interest that could unfairly benefit players contracted to that particular company. Besides the conflict of interest undertaking for all players and personnel, the player–agent accreditation and eligibility also need to be worked on. A certification of competency and a declaration of integrity ethics as well as veracity should be insisted upon prior to any player or personnel being represented by an individual or player/personnel representation entity. When the spot-fixing scandal broke out in May 2013, there were loud whispers within cricket circles of how Aditya Verma was closely linked to Modi and that his crusade against the BCCI–IPL was funded and morally supported by Modi.[10] When the story broke in 2015, Modi admitted his role in backing Verma but the latter disputed it, saying the initiative was entirely his own. No matter which story is accurate, the fact remains that a small, non-functional and virtually broke state federation for cricket in Bihar took on the behemoths of the BCCI–IPL, and took them all the way to the Supreme Court where it continues to challenge and trouble them. The IPL is in trouble because of it, and Srinivasan's conflict of interest has been highlighted and eliminated because of CAB's war of attrition. When the court was approached, no one knew just how far the Justice Mudgal Committee, the court, or later the Justice Lodha Committee would take the matter. Once the conflict of interest issues were raised by the Justice Mudgal Committee, the BCCI had reached the slippery slope, and continues to slip to this day.

The spot-fixing scandal led to two distinct focus areas for the court as it set out on its mission to clean the sport of cricket, and bring the BCCI–IPL to its heels. Although painted by the same brush by the court and its appointed committees, the two were peas from entirely different pods. The spot-fixing scandal opened the door for closer scrutiny into the matters of the BCCI and the IPL. Anyone who had a working knowledge of the BCCI was aware of the many different components where roles overlapped and decisions were made by individuals who managed to sit on both sides of the negotiating table for the same matter. Srinivasan became the court's poster child for all that was wrong with conflict of interest in cricket, but the matter extended beyond the very apparent clash of interest between being an administrator and of having a commercial arrangement with the board as a team owner. Modi certainly had strong opinions about it, and he let many of those known in the days after his exit from the IPL. The original conflict of interest dilemma was tackled by the court through its sanctioning of Srinivasan and the CSK. To get a clearer picture of how the conflict of interest was addressed by the court and subsequently tackled, it would be useful to look at the chronology of events. The Justice Mudgal Committee's two reports laid the foundation. The court took the IPL and the board to task. Over a series of hearings in November 2014, the court analysed and dissected the BCCI and the IPL against the backdrop of the report. It suggested that the CSK be terminated due to conflicts of interest, and recommended that the elections of the BCCI be conducted in a manner that allowed the board a clean start and perspective. These were merely observations but were telling. Then the court brought in the principles of natural justice, and the 'doctrine of public trust' which it felt applied. This principle and doctrine made the citizens of India the true plaintiffs against the ills of the IPL, and widened the parameters of scrutiny. In December 2014, the court became even more critical and cracked down harder on the conflict of interest issue. While Srinivasan continued to seek permission to contest the BCCI elections, the court continued to focus on the many conflicts facing the IPL. It centred its observations not only on Srinivasan and the CSK, but also started making direct inquiries of all who were subject to conflict of interest in the BCCI–IPL. The names of officials, administrators and cricketers that the board's counsel submitted in mid-December included the likes of Sourav Ganguly, Ravi Shastri and Sunil Gavaskar.[11] The court was not amused.

On 22 January 2015, the spot-fixing and conflict of interest verdict set the ball rolling for change. Srinivasan was asked to choose between the CSK and the BCCI, Clause 6.2.4 was struck down, and the Justice Lodha Committee was set up for acting on the ruling. On 14 July 2015, the Justice Lodha Committee announced its landmark decision, with the biggest development being the suspension of the CSK and the RR for two years.[12] The BCCI's and the IPL's response at that time was crucial. It was found wanting. The governing council announced its intention to comply with the order, but to analyse it closely, set up a working committee within it. This working committee required six weeks for analysis and would then submit its recommendations to the governing council. The council would then consider the recommendations, mull over them for some time, and then forward them to the board. It appeared to be an exercise in futility, given that there wasn't much leeway given to the league in the first place. The order also set into motion a series of moves by Srinivasan to offload the CSK from India Cements, and from him. These were the two controversial transfers which have been mentioned in Chapter 3.

Justice Lodha, when interviewed, hinted at how the governing council or the BCCI could, if they had so chosen, terminate the two franchises. The committee did not believe that its mandate included immersing itself in the contractual arrangement and acting as a party, but from its perspective suspension was merely a disciplinary move, and the board or the governing council could go beyond it. The IPL working group's scope included assessing the future of the two suspended franchises, as well as how best to ensure that the IPL remained a valuable and viable event for everyone. It showed reluctance, at least publicly, in terminating the suspended franchises. Unconfirmed reports indicated at the time that this was out of concern that the franchises would then successfully seek legal remedy for reinstatement and/or damages for wrongful termination. If that was indeed the reason the franchises were not terminated immediately, the board and the IPL working group lost out on their best chance at redemption and restoring integrity to the IPL. If ever there was a chance of the board being viewed favourably by the court and the Justice Lodha Committee, it would have had to terminate the franchises whose actions both had felt were egregious

enough to merit such an action. A termination by the board
of the CSK and the RR would in all likelihood have been
upheld by the court were the matter to appear before it.
To move towards degrees of separation from the conflict
of interest web that the IPL was trapped in, the board in
August had taken the positive step of announcing a conflict
of interest undertaking required for BCCI officials. That
move however was incomplete. A later clarification was
that current and former cricketers would not be required to
sign the undertaking. Not making it applicable to current
and former players was pointless and confusing. Over the
past few years, there had been numerous misgivings related
to the duality of roles that current and former cricketers had
in the current system. A strong and positive first step by the
board ought to have been a meritorious and consistent move
towards eradicating conflict of interest in cricket. It would
have shown how proactive the board was being, and would
have shown the court and the committees that it meant to
implement the directive it had received, and thereby would
have helped the IPL and cricket avoid further scrutiny. In
September 2015, the apex court struck down a plea by
the BCCI that sought a review of the verdict which had
invalidated clause 6.2.4, claiming that the review petition
made by the board's counsel had no merit.[13] Manohar, in
his second stint as president, has already announced his
plans to clamp down hard on conflict of interest, and has
circulated an even more detailed declaration form that is
sure to create tension with state associations. He has also
added more stringent auditing requirements and vigilance
regarding usage of the funds given by the board to state
associations. He has also brought current and former

players within the conflict of interest reparation drive, and is planning to ensure their compliance. Enforceability will be a big issue, and it remains to be seen if Manohar will achieve success, and how he will deal with rebellious state associations.

From any angle one looks at it, a blanket and uniform conflict of interest undertaking should be a requirement for anyone and everyone with a stake in cricket. As a player, former player, team owner, team personnel, sponsor, selector or administrator, a conflict of interest undertaking is a sign of good governance. The court's verdict in January put a stamp on how conflict of interest would no longer be tolerated. It left the two beleaguered franchises out in the cold, and it kept Srinivasan out of the race for the BCCI presidency. It also gave hope that the board and the league would function in a clean, accountable and transparent manner. The board's ombudsman has stated a mandate to clear conflict of interest complications, and the Justice Lodha Committee has created a comprehensive road map for how conflict of interest could be eliminated from cricket. The board, meanwhile, needs to continue to eradicate conflict of interest and put in place an absolutely transparent operating system.

The reason why conflict of interest hit the headlines rather than just being another example of unethical behaviour by the BCCI was due to the internal upheaval that the IPL had caused within the BCCI. The IPL, in many ways, is the catalyst for the disbanding of the boys' club that the BCCI had been for generations, and put the extremely stark differences into the public domain. Perhaps it was the ouster of Modi in 2010 that led to the eventual breakdown of confidentiality within the BCCI–IPL, but the seeds of discontent had been sowed many years earlier. It wasn't that the conflict of interest was new or any more harmful in the IPL than it had been in the BCCI before the IPL. It was just that due to the fame and fortune associated with the IPL, the stakes had got higher. So in the power game between the various personalities within the BCCI, grievances were more frequently aired on social media and in television interviews.

The most surprising aspects of the BCCI–IPL controversies—in particular regarding conflict of interest—are how a group of some of the most intelligent and successful individuals could independently fail to see that the level of interplay was bound to at some point be problematic.[14] This is an issue seen most frequently in sports administration scandals, and the BCCI–IPL had some head-scratching moments it could easily have nipped in the bud but didn't.[15] Anyone could see that the CSK was getting preferential treatment either by coincidence or intent. There were so many overlaps of India Cements beneficiaries across the IPL and the national team that it had become almost laughable. Let's look at this closely.

In 2011–12, Srinivasan was the president of the BCCI. The captain of his team, Dhoni, was also the captain of the Indian team, and a vice-president at India Cements. Four members of the CSK were in the Indian squad. And irrespective of whether it was due to merit or favouritism, it didn't reflect well on the team's owner. Suresh Raina, R. Ashwin, Murali Vijay and, later in 2012, Ravindra Jadeja, all have had extended runs in the playing eleven of the Indian team. The brand ambassador of the CSK until 2012, former India opener K. Srikkanth, also happened to be the national team selector. His son, Anirudha Srikkanth, was mostly a non-playing member of the CSK until Srikkanth Sr himself moved to a chief mentor's role in Sunrisers Hyderabad; his son has been a member of that team since 2013. Srikkanth Sr was one of the persons mentioned in the report submitted by the BCCI to the court of former players with conflict of interest. He had also been singled out for his role that clearly put him in a position of influence, and in a position to benefit the members of the team for which he was the brand ambassador or chief mentor.[16]

Srinivasan had always been excellent at multitasking, but his role in the IPL redefined the term 'involved'. At his peak, Srinivasan was the president of the BCCI, de facto president of the Tamil Nadu Cricket Association, chairman elect of the ICC, a member of the IPL governing council, and a team owner of the CSK. He technically sat on both sides of the table, and also presided over all cricket-related matters. There is no fathomable way in which Srinivasan could honestly claim that there wasn't a dichotomy with regard to his priorities in his multiple roles. There was so much overlap between Srinivasan's network and that of the BCCI–IPL that it bordered on the absurd. Even players in the national team and the CSK were office bearers or employees of India Cements. This rampant conflict of interest was damaging to the IPL and to the BCCI. But this wasn't the only variant of conflict of interest that has eroded the reputation and goodwill of the IPL and the BCCI.

Politicians being active in both the IPL and the board is another failing on the conflict of interest front. It would be unfair to say that having politicians administer cricket is bad for the IPL. On the contrary, politicians would by default be good administrators. The problem is that they have multiple roles and interests, and more importantly, having politicians as administrators takes the focus and priority away from the goals and results of what the IPL and the BCCI are supposed to accomplish. It puts an unnecessary stigma on the reputation and success, in this case of the IPL, and creates an automatic conflict of interest between what a public official is supposed to achieve in his/her official role and what he/she is expected to achieve in their administrative role. It also impacts the priority when a full-time elected public official is at the helm of the board or of the IPL—it leads to the question whether the IPL or the board will get the core attention it requires and deserves. A further challenge is the extended tenure and extent of influence that politicians have maintained in the BCCI–IPL. If these arguments don't convince the reader, this statement should: In the history of the IPL till date, the politician–IPL nexus has not produced a single positive outcome. Even now, the issue of politicians involved with Indian cricket comes up frequently. Recently, Ian Chappell, the legendary former Australian captain and a respected television commentator, mentioned the fact that there were too many politicians involved with Indian cricket.[17]

The IPL's architect Modi has himself been caught in numerous conflicts of interest allegations. The most recent allegation almost caused Sushma Swaraj, a Cabinet minister, and Vasundhara Raje, the chief minister of Rajasthan, their positions. Increasingly, there is today a push for the IPL and to a certain extent the board, to be administered by a former cricketer with impeccable credentials and some experience in administration. The court made its opinion known in 2014 when it appointed Gavaskar as the interim head of the IPL. Sourav Ganguly is now the president of the Cricket Association of Bengal, succeeding the late BCCI president Jagmohan Dalmiya, and it is expected that one day he will lead the BCCI as well.

For now however, this is what is important. The line between cricket and politics in India has blurred, and there needs to be a clear bifurcation where politicians and bureaucrats should not actively be involved. Especially in running or governing entities such as the IPL. There are simply not enough pros as against the cons.

The reason why politicians would be interested in running cricket is perhaps due to the similarity of position, power and administration. This is not the norm globally in sports—politicians in successful sporting nations are only rarely directly involved with the governance or administration of sports bodies. In the rarest of rare circumstances, such as during the Salt Lake City Winter Olympics of 2002, are politicians brought in to stem crises and chart a plausible way forward. There, former governor of Massachusetts and future presidential nominee Mitt Romney were brought in to help administer the Winter Olympics after a bribery scandal threatened to have the event cancelled altogether. That however was an emergency move, and a temporary one. There are other examples where former athletes-turned-politicians are appointed to head sports committees as they provide a unique combination of skills and experiences.

With their wide image dissemination, sportspersons often take up public roles across the world. Even in India that has been the case. But a politician with no clear connection to cricket should probably be prevented. It won't be easy to do, and among politicians it will be a very unpopular move. It is, however, necessary. Theoretically, it can be done by issuing a directive that no public or government official should be eligible to contest for a cricket administration position at the district, state or national level. The only exception should be for the rarest of rare cases where a politician or bureaucrat has in his/her lifetime represented India as a sportsperson. This isn't foolproof but it can definitely reduce the influx of politicians with no connection to cricket who keep other qualified candidates out. For those politicians or bureaucrats who either retire or choose to be full-time cricket officials, there must be a cooling-off period to ensure that no conflict of interest remains before they take on such a responsibility. A natural corollary would be to require the immediate resignation of a former politician elected or appointed to the board or to any of the IPL's councils after the cooling-off period, upon the individual returning to a public position at any time.

Legally and constitutionally, this may not be easy. The challenges include the constitutional bar on discrimination against a particular class of individuals, as well as the difficulty in defining who or what a politician/public official/government official is, and then monitoring and enforcing the restriction. To eliminate politicians or bureaucrats altogether would no doubt be discriminatory, constitutionally difficult to ensure, and above all else, counterproductive. It is also unnecessary to go to that far an extent since a directive by the Justice Lodha Committee to this effect may be enough which is then accepted by the Supreme Court. It would, of course, be unfair to those politicians who appear to be doing solid foundation work, but in all fairness they ought to choose one of the two positions and focus their entire attention towards the direction they choose. To close additional loopholes, lifetime honorary positions or 'advisory' roles in the IPL or the BCCI should also be eliminated. Politics and the BCCI–IPL have just not been a successful pairing, analogous to red wine and fish or single malt and tonic water. This has, in many ways, been an opportunity lost for the IPL and for the BCCI. Ever since the spot-fixing scandal and the conflict of interest controversies occurred, the BCCI has been put on notice to fix itself and the IPL. It didn't do either. In fact, not until the Justice Lodha Committee came out with its order did any moves towards solidity and transparency even occur. In all these discussions on conflict of interest, and the coming down hard by the judiciary on the workings of the BCCI–IPL, one crucial aspect has been forgotten. It has to do with the fact that the BCCI is the most important member of the ICC. The IPL is the most important component today of the BCCI. Therefore, one shouldn't make the mistake of assuming that if a crackdown occurs, and the Supreme Court decides to take matters into its own hands, the BCCI–IPL will necessarily comply.

The board's recourse, if the Justice Lodha Committee's recommendations and the Supreme Court's directives completely cut its wings, could be one that will have long-lasting repercussions for the IPL as we know it. To think that a board as influential as the BCCI in terms of the world cricket order, or as wealthy, has no options is a fatal mistake. The board, which now, of course, has unprecedented leverage in the ICC, has recourse which could separate it from the direct purview of the court and indirectly, of the Indian public. If a drastic step was to be taken, here is how that would go down.

The BCCI could feel aggrieved at being singled out for what could be deemed a punitive detoxification. If the worst-case scenario for the BCCI unfolds, where its nominated or elected committee members are disqualified from contesting future elections, certain franchises are directed to be terminated, and the IPL itself becomes of ambiguous viability, the BCCI may deliberate and activate its options.

The first and most intuitive rectification the board could seek, regardless of whether or not it emerges victorious in the matter, is to assign the commercial rights of the IPL to a private limited entity that has the sanction of the BCCI, but very little link other than that. This is a theme I have touched upon throughout this book. Had this been the original framework of the league, rather than establishing it as a subcommittee of the BCCI, it could have functioned relatively unhindered as a for-profit private league. It would still have been recognized as 'official cricket' in the form of a domestic event, and it is unlikely that the conflict of interest would have been as barbed an argument, given that the executive body of the board would not be directly involved with the corpus or commercials of the league. The board could have been accused of being opportunistic, capitalistic even, but many of the grievances that the public and judiciary have against it would have been nullified to a certain extent. Certainly, this would have been in line with international best practices, and interestingly, some recently launched professional sports leagues have followed in principle a similar corporate structure.

A second course of action and one which is perhaps more extreme and worrying would be if the BCCI decides that the constant scrutiny and involvement by the judiciary and legislature could render it untenable to continue as a national sports federation. The board could then look at establishing itself as a private entity that fields cricket teams, organizes cricket events, and most importantly, it will apply to the ICC for official sanction and accreditation. The reason why this is possible is that the BCCI is an extremely vital and powerful member of the ICC, and it continues to have excellent relations with the world's governing body for cricket. Even the recent move to reverse the Big Three phenomena in the ICC doesn't take away from the fact that the board is the dominant cricket association in the world. So in all probability, the ICC and its members would give it permission, and its experience and network would ensure that it will be able to develop and run cricket with more success than any competing body. An aspect that further strengthens this argument is that cricket isn't, and in all likelihood won't be, represented at the Olympics or Commonwealth Games, and BCCI has chosen not to field a squad for the Asiad; so for all intents and purposes, the BCCI will probably not require accreditation from the IOC or be obliged to follow the Olympic Charter, or that of any other global governing body except the ICC. And of even more relevance, if the only sanctioning body is the ICC, any punishment meted out to the board under the ICC's anti-corruption regulations would probably be heard once more by the ICC's panel, rather than just implementing the directive of the committee or the courts.

The BCCI's concerns, if it pursues the above, are the following: a possible restricted supply of cricket stadiums made available to it in India, and if the prevention of sporting fraud bill becomes a law, it will not be allowed to officially field the 'Indian team' or 'Team India' as an unaccredited Indian federation. The former issue could be solved if the board uses its networks to rent the stadiums on a commercial basis from the state federations, or in the longer term, create privately owned stadiums/ infrastructure. The latter issue of naming rights could be resolved by creative wordplay, provided, of course, that the bill becomes a law, rendering this necessary. If push comes to shove, the IPL could even be moved on a permanent basis outside of India—not ideal, but an option. It will be called by another name, but it will just be a new package for an established product. What could work even further to its advantage is that the elected members of the this cricket federation may just be proxy members of the BCCI–IPL, and thus allow the league to exist as it is, while on the surface administering cricket differently.

If the board's position is made untenable in what it could, perhaps reasonably, view as a witch-hunt against it, it will review its options. They may be unpopular and they will be complicated, but they are possible. If pushed into a corner, it may just exercise them. After all, almost two entire seasons of the IPL—2009 and 2014—have been conducted abroad, in South Africa and the UAE respectively.

It is a short event, and moving the machinery for less than two months is hardly a Herculean task, especially given that there are no concrete reasons forcing the IPL to be conducted in India in the first place. In fact, already many of the franchises play 'home' games at different stadiums in different cities than which they belong to. The RR doesn't play a single game in Jaipur or anywhere in Rajasthan. So, of course, it can be done. Not being a part of the Indian sports structure doesn't hurt the IPL primarily because cricket isn't an Olympic sport, and increasingly, T20 is becoming a private enterprise.

In its current frame of mind, the board doesn't seem to be keen to do anything that radical. If anything, it seems keen to be compliant and eliminate conflict of interest. The IPL appears to be getting reined in, and soon a conclusive decision will be made about how those conflicted will be handled. There is hope yet for conflict of interest to be controlled without external interference. Along with conflict of interest, the board needs to fix the current player allocation system as well—the players' auction.

The Players' Auction

The evolution of the IPL is, of course, unique when compared to any other professional sports league in the world. Cricket is dominated by the international calendar, and therefore the US professional sports leagues cannot be emulated—especially the National Football League and Major League Baseball (MLB). Due to a loaded international calendar, the IPL, for the most part, is the shortest league in terms of duration and overall time commitment, especially for the teams that don't advance beyond the group stages and qualify for the CLT20; or at least, did until the CLT20 was put to rest in 2015. If anything, the IPL isn't a league at all, as will be discussed in greater detail in the next chapter. In addition, the IPL has the enviable situation whereby the world's best cricketers and overall talent pool, with very few exceptions, are available for selection, or at least until recently, they were.

What the IPL doesn't have yet however is a player selection, retention and transfer process that is sophisticated, dynamic or robust enough to keep pace with the rapidly evolving (and escalating) pay scales and related requirements to ensure parity and equitable distribution. If there is one aspect of the IPL that requires immediate change, it is the IPL's much-maligned player auction. A system designed to select players on the basis of market forces, the auction is conceivably meant to determine the players' value, along the lines of a player draft like the NFL, the MLB or any other league.

The problem with the existing auction system is that it resembles a 'fantasy league' in terms of how it operates. The move from fantasy to reality is imperative, and the first step that needs to be taken is to introduce the draft (as discussed below) and all the associated machinery that makes global sports leagues unique in and of themselves.

It would be fair to say that in most leagues, player drafts are sophisticated processes that have evolved over decades. They are determined on the basis of the players' representatives/associations negotiating certain salary floors (on a player-by-player basis), and salary caps (on a team-by-team basis) with the commissioner's office, and also with individual teams. The outcome of these negotiations determines, among other things, the range and strictly mandated league-specific regulations governing drafts, team selection, salary caps, player loans and trades, salary arbitration, and free agency. This process is known as 'collective bargaining'. From the IPL's perspective, this concept is somewhat futuristic, since an authorized IPL Players' Association does not exist, and may take some time to evolve.

Player auction 2015 (IPL VIII)

Even in 2015, the auction remained an economic anomaly. Yet, for reasons best known to its officials, it remained a mainstay, and an apparently unavoidable necessity. The 2015 auction was a perfect example of how things went wrong because of this outdated and impractical player selection mechanism.

If the auction was intended to level IPL VIII's playing field, it failed. The auction spurs deviations that increase the dichotomy between teams entirely reliant on the auction for strengthening their squads and those who were well set, given that their squads were already almost at full strength due to player retentions from the previous season. Player retentions, of course, is one of the primary reasons why there is so little parity in the IPL, which favours the haves and sinks the have-nots. There is no point whatsoever in having an auction, and at the same time allowing teams to retain a number of their best players year after year, outside of the auction. Take the example of the CSK, arguably the most successful IPL franchise. Of course, the franchise's current status leads one to believe that a lot more was at play, but from the perspective of performance, the CSK's core team had remained unchanged from the first couple of seasons onwards. Without primary dependence on the auction, it has been far easier for teams like the CSK to field great teams built around its core. Teams that have retained players for eight seasons and counting, simply have an advantage over those that are dependent on the auction. The Delhi team is the perfect example of a team that has consistently been dependent on the auction, and has consequently suffered.

The retention right has been inefficient since its inception and continues to be so because it can artificially inflate the wages owed to the retained players, as it is also outside the purview of the salary cap. It is a right which takes several coveted players outside the economic marketplace of competitive demand and supply, and reduces the probability of there being a level playing field. Already good teams could become great because they retained the core of their team at fixed wages from the standpoint of salary cap, but could negotiate individual salaries with each retained player at a rate that fell outside the parameters of salary cap. So for the auction prior to IPL VII in 2014, for teams such as Delhi Daredevils or Kings XI Punjab, it served merely as a qualified fresh start, since twenty-four players had already been taken out of the auction through retention, and another nine to ten players were effectively out of reach if the right to match option was exercised. The right to match option was given to a franchise which had the option to bid for a player who had represented the franchise the previous season but had not been retained by it. During the auction, if another franchise made a bid for the player, the franchise with the right to match card could use the card to retain the player at the same amount as the highest bid the player had received during the auction. So, for 2014, not only was it an extremely limited auction, it also lent a feel of preferential treatment being given to the traditional powerhouse franchises, in a setting where transparency had been compromised. It was a familiar theme and was repeated again the following season. In the real world, this is untenable as an economics model, and unviable from an accountability parameter.

In the past as well, player retentions have raised question marks when it came to creative methods employed by franchises who would provide supplementary income opportunities for players outside the realm of the IPL wages so as to ensure the salary cap isn't breached, yet the players remain contracted to the team that covet them. A prime example was the two-pronged engagement that the RCB had with Chris Gayle in 2012. Gayle is, along with A.B. deVilliers, the most valuable international cricketer in the IPL. Gayle has scored 3199 runs in just eighty-two matches in the IPL at an average of over 46 and a strike rate of 153. He has five centuries, eighteen fifties and 230 sixes in his IPL career. He even has sixteen wickets from his part-time off-spin bowling. He won the Orange Cap in successive seasons—2011 and 2012—for being the leading run scorer. Having been passed over during the 2011 auction, he was signed as a replacement for Dirk Nannes who withdrew, at the same wages as Nannes had been signed for, US$650,000 on a one-year contract. It was widely assumed that Gayle would be the highest priced player in the 2012 auction, with estimates hovering in the US$2 million range, which was the total salary purse that teams had for the supplementary auction. On 20 January 2012, however, it was announced that Gayle would be the brand ambassador for the UB Group's UK arm, as the endorser for Whyte & Mackay, UB's flagship whiskey. It was rumoured that the deal was for US$2 million, and shortly thereafter, the RCB announced that they had retained Gayle for two more seasons for an undisclosed amount. Other teams were aggrieved at this sweetening of the salary pie through supplemental sponsorship deals, and once again it highlighted the challenge of creating a level playing field primarily on the basis of a salary cap that had so many loopholes. The entire concept of player retention has single-handedly led to lopsided team structures, and finally the newly formed governing council in 2015 announced a modification to the retention policy from 2017 onwards, limiting the number of Indian capped players to two, and even overseas players to two per team. Although a small step, it certainly indicates how the skewed retention policy has favoured teams like the CSK, and perhaps it is because of the CSK's falling out of favour that this reworking of the retention policy has been implemented. Is it a case of too little too late? Time will tell.

In the meantime, let's look at the 2015 auction to see how dependent teams like Delhi Daredevils were impacted. The two biggest and most controversial acquisitions, Yuvraj Singh and Dinesh Karthik, came at exorbitant cost. Yuvraj cost INR16 crore and Karthik cost INR10.5 crore. The cost was imposed due to artificial price floors caused by squad retentions and consequently, scarcity of talent supply. It was clearly not because of the players' performances for the national team, or for their IPL teams the previous years. Yuvraj, for someone of his calibre and ability, has had a middling IPL career, with seven seasons and ninety-eight matches yielding 2099 runs at an average of 25.28, and strike rate of 129. His bowling has produced thirty-five wickets at an economy of 7.27 runs per over, and an average of 28. His bowling in 2015 was a vanishing aspect of his game, and his fielding too wasn't nearly as sharp as it was at his peak. Compare his IPL career to an Indian player in the CSK—Suresh Raina. Raina is admittedly one of the best T20 players India has ever produced, and has been with the CSK since 2008. He has played in 132 matches in the IPL, amassing 3699 runs at an average of 34.25 and a strike rate of over 139. He also has twenty-four wickets at an average of 39 and an economy of 7.24. His performance is stellar, yet, because of his being retained by the CSK each year, he earns much less than those who are in the auction. That's hardly a performance-driven model.

The market dynamics were thus voided and led to the inability of the acquiring teams to assess the correct permutation and combination to put together its squad prior to the actual auction. Like every other year, the 2015 auction had turned into a game of chance rather than strategy. Of the INR87.6 crore spent in total at the auction, approximately 30 per cent, or INR26.5 crore was spent on Yuvraj and Karthik. This in an auction that featured the following players, all of whom were among the 282 unsold players who did not even get a single bid:

Hashim Amla, Cameron White, Tillakaratne Dilshan, Marlon Samuels, Kumar Sangakkara, Mahela Jayawardene, Brad Hodge, Cheteshwar Pujara and Ross Taylor. Not a single bid for any of these players. It is virtually impossible to justify this flawed mechanism any longer.

With the auction being what it is, it's only fair that the reserve price concept is also equally inefficient. Players lose the opportunity to participate in the IPL due to the setting up of a reserve price that is at odds with their value to the teams. Reserve prices need to be kept flexible for later rounds if the players are unsold after the initial round of bids, allowing the players to reduce them so as to allow themselves a fair shot at being acquired. The cost of overestimating one's talents and value is often too high in the current system, especially for domestic players who often don't have professional representation to advise them.

The Uncapped Player Auction ought to have had a uniform cap for each player, and selection should have been through a lottery draft. This way, teams that are rebuilding would have a better chance at acquiring future talent without a bidding war. In the 2015 auction, two uncapped players—Shreyas Iyer and K.C. Cariappa—arbitrarily earned INR5 crore between them based purely on potential, twenty-five times over their combined reserve price. While Iyer performed extremely well for Delhi, Cariappa barely got a chance to spin the Eden Gardens crowd into a frenzy. Such a wide and arbitrary range with vastly contrasting results has to be addressed. A uniform cap and lottery draft should correct this.

Take another example in 2015 of the randomness of the player assessment and/or valuation. As Delhi was the most active team in the 2015 auction, let's look at its two new acquisitions. Angelo Mathews, the Sri Lankan captain, and Albie Morkel of South Africa have had similar batting and bowling averages through their IPL careers. Morkel has played in all seven seasons of the IPL leading in to 2015, and in eighty matches had scored 872 runs at an average of 22.94, and taken eighty wickets at an average of 27.30. Mathews had played in three IPL seasons and had skipped IPL 2014 for national duty. In thirty-five matches, Mathews had scored 548 runs at an average of 24.90, and taken twenty wickets at an average of 38.85. Further, given the Tamil Nadu government's stance on not allowing Sri Lankan players to play IPL matches in Chennai, Mathews in 2015 would not have been available for any match Delhi played in Chennai.

Morkel's career had been somewhat on the wane while Mathews as the captain of the Sri Lankan team was clearly a more attractive proposition; but the auction results were staggering. The pricing differential between the two was twenty-five times, with Morkel acquired at his reserve price of INR30 lakh and Mathews for the auction's third highest amount of INR7.5 crore. Factoring in the otherwise blanket shunning of the Sri Lankan players at the auction, this decision highlighted the game theory imperfections that has made the auction system fraught with inefficiencies.

It is the embarrassment of mass bypassing or rejection of successful cricketers, and the additional time spent on broadcasting an auction where a majority of the players are passed over that need correcting. The IPL ought to have ensured an eligibility standard for players who made themselves available for the auction. Players ought to meet the minimum threshold of points accumulated, based on the interest of each franchise, which would allot points to players it was interested in, in advance of the auction. Only after meeting the threshold should their names have entered into the actual auction itself. It was telling that in the 2015 auction, less than one in every five players was actually picked, leading to a total of sixty-seven players from the 349 who made themselves available. The 2016 auction was again a chip off the old block. As many as 351 cricketers were included in the auction and just ninety-four were sold, with just over 26 per cent of the players in the auction actually being selected. The sold players featured sixty-six Indians and twenty-eight overseas cricketers, and Shane Watson was the highest money earner going for INR 9.5 crore to the RCB.

Of course, the two franchises which at the time were not suspended—the CSK and the RR— had minimal parts to play in the auction, having retained their strong squads almost in its entirety. That by itself ought to have worried the powers that be, but, of course, it didn't. That is, until later in 2015, when the change in control led to revisions in the IPL rules, albeit minimal ones.

The secret auction and how it hurt the integrity of selection

Auction is, of course, a bad idea, and the player retention policy an even worse one. But when it comes to a complete breakdown in transparency, accountability and parity due to one single step, it would have to be the so-called tiebreaker 'secret player's auction', and its completely discretionary power to allocate a resource on the basis of deep pockets—and in the process enrich the already wealthy central IPL coffers. The 'secret player's auction' was a new low, even for the IPL. Modelled on the secret auction at charity raffles, its idea was that if a highly coveted player was pursued with equal enthusiasm by two or more teams to a point where the maximum price for the player had been reached, then a tiebreaker would be used to determine the player's ultimate destination. At the third IPL auction, two players were so hotly pursued—Kieron Pollard and Shane

Bond—that after maxing out the bid ceiling of US$750,000 for each, the franchises submitted secret bids to determine the winner of the tiebreaker. Modi at the time announced that the secret bid was to be known only by him and the successful bidders. Not exactly the foundation for a transparent player allotment methodology. In 2012, Modi mentioned in a television interview that the tiebreaker was meant to level the playing field, but did not specifically address why it was kept secret. It wouldn't be a surprise if many of the franchises were unhappy with the tiebreaker rule as it appeared to favour those with deep pockets, and also kept the sole discretion and power in the hands of Modi. The fact that the entire amount of the secret bid went to the BCCI and not to the player didn't help the perception of this process. The last player to be allocated through this colossal breakdown of transparent practices was none other than Ravindra Jadeja, who in 2012 was pursued by the CSK and the DC, both maxing out their entire salary purses of US$2 million; the CSK went on to win the secret tiebreaker. By then, Modi was no longer at the helm of the IPL, and Srinivasan was the president of the BCCI. Even if the entire process was absolutely legitimate, the secrecy with which it was shrouded was extremely avoidable. Thankfully, the methodology has not been used in auctions since 2012.

On the topic of Jadeja, he is one of the first known violators of IPL regulations, creating a stir in 2009 and ending up suspended for that season due to his actions. In all honesty it probably wasn't his fault, and was actually a result of the ambiguity that young players with limited exposure to processes would understandably face. Jadeja was contracted to play for the RR and in the first season of the IPL had done extremely well as a young talent. Well enough that he felt he ought to renegotiate and speak with other teams in the IPL for season two. This however was not allowed, and no one who understood the nuances of the rules and regulations was able to explain this to Jadeja. The background of this was that the governing council had banned any player agents from representing their clients' interests in the IPL, unofficially to prevent the players having much leverage in discussions, and also to make the contract signing a mere formality rather than a full-drawn negotiation. There is to this day no players' association where cricketers can seek advice and support as a joint body of individuals. With zero leverage and zero knowledge, Jadeja was suspended for an entire season thanks to his desire to negotiate. It was one of the many grey areas in the IPL rules and regulations, and it mostly impacted uncapped Indian players. Had the IPL merely emulated the US leagues, it could have introduced a mechanism for remuneration, known as 'salary arbitration', as a contractual feature that players could have mobilized if such an option existed within the framework of their contracts.

Going back to the auction-related controversies. The IPL and especially the CSK have had some other newsworthy controversies with regard to the auction. In 2011, Mumbai Indians and other franchises were at the receiving end of a completely arbitrary and last-minute change to the upcoming auction. The auction was meant to feature predetermined sets of players in each round on the basis of skill sets and/or reputation. So the marquee players would have formed one set, specialist batsmen another, specialist bowlers the third, all-rounders the fourth, and so on. The order of the auction, as the franchises were informed, was to be decided at the auction itself, selected at random. This, it was stated, would enhance transparency and accountability, while ensuring a level playing field. The franchises were therefore aggrieved when on the eve of the auction they were informed that the random nature of the auction was to be replaced by a predefined order in sets that did not necessarily feature players of similar skill sets or specializations. The predefined sets and line-up were not shared with the franchises as a whole. There were concerns that certain individuals or franchises would have been privy to the information and the line-up, helping them significantly in their selection preparation, and in budgeting for the auction in the optimal way. The CSK had the decided advantage of having the BCCI president-elect participating in all the governing council meetings that decided the processes, including the auction order; at the same time, Srinivasan's company sat on the franchise's side as team owners. Many of the franchises at the time were said to be unhappy with this development, and said that no justification was given for changing the random selection process to a predefined order. Mumbai Indians were the most vocal, and immediately sent off a letter to the governing council expressing its unhappiness and requesting an explanation for what could easily be deemed to be a case of unilateral authorization. The presumption, whether correct or not, was that this was done to benefit the CSK. No answers were forthcoming, and yet another example of the exploitable nature of the auction was before the franchises and the general public.[1] Nothing, of course, was done about it.

This controversy was followed by another Modi snippet in February 2012 where he claimed in a television interview that he had been pressurized in 2009 to rig the auction in a manner that benefited the CSK, allowing it the opportunity to buy Andrew Flintoff. Modi said that he had rigged the auction to ensure that J.P. Duminy was placed ahead of Flintoff as was Shaun Tait, leading to Mumbai Indians and Rajasthan Royals spending their allowances on each player respectively, leaving them unable to afford Flintoff who eventually went to the CSK for a record amount (at the time) of US$1.55 million. Modi also claimed that all of the franchises had been coerced by the board to not buy any of the Pakistani players placed in the auction in 2009 as a fallout of the Mumbai terror attacks that soured relations between India and Pakistan. It's clear that the auction was misused and even if it wasn't, it was an opaque and inefficient way of allocating the players. There is no justification to retain this, and the longer the BCCI does so, it only leads to questions about the authenticity and integrity of the player selection process.

Assume now that given the various developments off-pitch, the governing council and the BCCI decide to do things the right way. And by right way, I mean transparently and as per global best practices. In that case, the auction needs to be replaced with a player draft. A draft that is very similar to what has been set out below, which has been modified for the IPL.

What are drafts?

Drafts are a mechanism used by leagues to ensure parity among teams in a systematic manner.

Basis indicators for the proposed IPL Draft

The proposed IPL Draft is meant to replace the existing auction system employed by the IPL. The draft will be a hybrid model borrowing from North American and European leagues, and could be implemented in IPL X or IPL XI. The IPL will need to rework its salary cap (explained below in point 1), and certain pre-draft exceptions (as explained below in point 2) can be enforced. The draft itself will be for all the players who have made themselves available for the IPL, and the players will be placed in the draft on the basis of IPL seniority and international stature (marquee players). The draft will be divided into sessions and rounds within those sessions, and the teams will be allotted draft picks on the basis of previous years' performance, and a lottery system (explained below in point 5). There will be a standardized allocation of time between picks and between sessions. The salary floors will be allocated for each session and round, and will be stipulated by the governing council or the commissioner/chairman's office, to ensure parity and level playing fields. Players will be selected on the basis of draft picks, and there shall be no mention of the amount each player shall make during the draft itself. Market forces will determine the value of a player, therefore ensuring the selection of meritorious players in the earliest rounds and sessions of the draft. Ideally, the draft will take place every three years.

1. Salary cap

First of all however, one must rework the existing salary cap structure. The salary cap could be a certain percentage (say, 10 per cent) of the net revenues derived from the central revenue pool (including central revenue sponsorships), revenues from broadcast rights, and from the IPL's share of gate receipts. The first and critical change that must be introduced is that a 'soft' salary cap should be implemented. A 'soft' salary cap has three components: (i) a fixed ceiling for each team's payroll/player wages; (ii) exceptions on the basis of standardized bonus clauses (discussed below in point 6); and (iii) three additional exemptions on the basis of unique skills that each franchise requires.

Therefore, if US$15 million is the salary cap, with the exclusion of said exceptions, each franchisee must adhere to this salary cap for the entire team's retainer payroll. However, the floors and ceilings of the retainer component will depend upon which round the player is picked in the draft. It will not apply to the pre-draft exceptions (explained below in point 2), nor will it apply to performance and other threshold bonuses that each team can factor into its contracts with the players.

There should also be an 'uncapped' component to the salary cap. At least 15 per cent of the salary cap must be spent on Indian players with or without IPL experience, but who have not yet been selected to represent India. Failure to utilize this component of the salary cap will result in penalties such as a team forgoing the subsequent draft's picks.

2. Pre-draft exceptions

2.1 Franchise Player (FP): For the player whose intangible contributions can enhance the franchise's performance or intrinsic value, the FP tag will result in a 15 per cent higher retainer than that of the next highest paid player in the team. However, the 15 per cent component shall be exempt from the salary cap. Each team can retain one player pre-draft subject to the FP exemption.

2.2 Future Star (FS): A team can activate this exception for an Indian player with more than three seasons, and less than six seasons of IPL experience. Only one such player can be tagged with this exception, if the team so chooses to do so prior to the draft. The FS shall be given the league-stipulated maximum retainer amount, with the difference between the previous contractual amount and the revised league-mandated amount not falling under the salary cap.

2.3 Rookie: A team can activate this exception for an Indian player who is less than twenty-two years old at the time the contract is signed, and with less than three seasons of IPL experience. This player, due to his unique positioning and skills, shall earn a retainer of 50 per cent more than the previous season, provided the player is considered 'uncapped' as per IPL's present definition of uncapped players. The 50 per cent premium will not fall within the salary cap. A team can activate this exception prior to the draft only for a player already within the team roster. If the player has already represented the Indian team before the opening of the exemption window, this exemption will not be applicable, and the player may enter the draft.

3. The draft

The pre-draft exceptions must be signed up during the exemption declaration deadline (EDD). The EDD shall be fourteen days prior to the draft being conducted. Once the pre-draft exceptions have been signed by the EDD, a list of available players per session will be circulated to the franchisees/teams. This list will be confidential, and all players on this list who do not get selected in a session will automatically get moved to the following session. The placement and positioning of players in the draft will be in terms of IPL seniority and overall 'marquee' status. One important change from the existing system in the IPL is to determine 'seniority' in terms of experience in IPL seasons, not in terms of age or first-class-cricket seniority. Prior to each cycle of the draft, a cricketer who has significant international experience but has been unable to participate in the IPL due to injury or international commitments can apply to the IPL governing council or the commissioner's office for a seniority exemption. The governing council can at its sole discretion decide to approve or decline the players' request.

4. The draft process

It is important to conduct the IPL draft in a manner that is equitable and systematic. Each draft will be divided into sessions and rounds within those sessions. There will be ten selections per round, and three rounds per session. Each round shall be one pick per team. After each pick, the team that must choose next will be put on the clock for three minutes in total before making its decision. The time allotted between picks can be reduced for entire sessions and rounds in a descending order.

The total number of rounds and sessions will depend on how many players are required to complete the rosters of all the teams. During the draft, there should be no mention of how much each pick is likely to earn—thereby eliminating the auction component. Each session will have its salary floors (and possibly ceilings), subject to the fixed component of the salary cap. The salary cap and salary floors will be decided at least one month prior to the draft. If a player is chosen in a particular round or session, the team can incentivize his contract within the parameters of the salary cap and bonuses. But at no point can the player's contract be for a value that is less than the league-stipulated salary floors on the basis of the round and session in which the player is picked. The only exception can be if the player is put on 'waivers' at the end of the draft, and voluntarily agrees to sign on as a free agent with any team that approaches him during the 'waiver period'. Such free-agent signings will be allowed for a period of one week following the draft's conclusion.

5. Lottery system

The teams will be allotted draft picks on the basis of a lottery system. Only teams that fail to qualify for the play-offs/semi-finals shall be eligible for the lottery picks in the next draft cycle. To ensure that performance levels are maintained, the lottery picks will be chosen randomly for the following draft cycle in a transparent process prior to the actual draft. Draft picks for the teams that qualify for the semi-finals shall form seven to ten picks in each round of Session 1. Session 2 picks and onward will be determined by lottery in a transparent process, irrespective of how the team fared in the previous cycle. The IPL governing council should set guidelines to ensure that teams can trade up or trade down for the following years' draft selections during the trading window for the current year. This will be beneficial for all the parties concerned.

6. Bonus clauses

Players shall be classified based on the positions they play: bowlers, batsmen, all-rounders, including wicketkeepers. Each category has benchmarks, and if a player meets the threshold criterion, he shall be eligible for a bonus that will fall outside the salary cap. This will not be a component of guaranteed incentives but will be performance-based and objective. Individual excellence (performance-based) and team success shall determine bonus criterion, and shall form the flexible portion of the soft salary cap structure. They will be stipulated by the league. The player lists prepared for the draft will also mention the players in position-wise categories. These would help in determining bonus parameters and unique skills.

7. Supplemental draft

The long-term model could be one where in every three seasons, there will be a comprehensive draft, comprising all the individuals who have not been signed on under the exceptions, or who have been part of a supplemental draft as described below. During the two interim off years, there should be a two-round supplemental draft. The first round should be a supplemental draft round for meritorious individuals who have not been part of the IPL in prior seasons, but have represented their respective countries. The contracts that they sign shall at no point extend beyond the next scheduled comprehensive draft. The second round shall be a rookie draft round, for Indian 'uncapped' players who shall be inducted into the IPL through an open selection process. The salary cap and floors can be predetermined by the IPL, and communicated to the franchisees/teams prior to the supplemental draft.

8. Player loans and trades

Borrowing from European league systems, player trades and loans, subject to all parties agreeing to the arrangement, could be a key component for optimizing synergies.

8.1 **Loans:** Player loans will be very useful in the IPL, as teams that are no longer competitive from the perspective of participation in the semi-finals, can loan their players to contenders, subject to the parties concerned agreeing to the terms and conditions that govern player loans. In most other leagues or sports, such an idea would have been dismissed as too utopian. But in the IPL, the omnipotent nature of the central league which controls all that transpires within it can actually be used to benefit the teams, the players and the fans. So the player and the two teams involved in the process must agree to remuneration and competition stipulations as per the governing body (ICC), or the league rules. The receiving team will take on the obligation of the players' pro rata retainers and bonus components for that particular season of the IPL. Also, a league-stipulated loan fee will be provided to the lending team by the recipient team. A percentage (say, 20 per cent) from the loan fee will be provided to the player to incentivize the loan.

In the IPL, this is a win-win for all, provided the loan meets the regulations and compliances. The player will have an opportunity to showcase his potential and boost his performance during the semi-finals, and to also be part of a contending team. The receiving team can fill in roster gaps to become more competitive for that particular season. The lending team will be able to offset its payroll expenses by loaning the players. Unlike the issues teams face in football leagues, there is no real conflict in the IPL because of its unique positioning and short duration. Besides, the rights to the player remain with the lending team, as soon as the borrowing teams' season concludes. The league will gain in terms of levels of competition and the calibre of the players in the contending teams. And, of course, for the fans and TRP ratings, teams loaded with talent and superstars make for far more exciting post-season matches. It is important however to ensure that the loan deadlines are clearly demarcated. Therefore, the 'loan window' must only be during the period between the conclusion of the IPL regular season, and before the commencing of the post-season play-offs.

8.2 Trades: Player trades are more complicated to structure and enforce, and can only be implemented effectively once the trade regulations are clearly stipulated. Also, it's imperative that the trade windows and deadlines are strictly adhered to. It will also require the IPL players' association to be established and effective. In essence, it's more than a step further than a player loan to another team. In a league such as the IPL, player trades must be synced with longer-term option contracts, and the concept of restricted and unrestricted free agency. There will also need to be a trade fee cap, and the concept of 'waivers' must also be implemented. Assigning the contracts by one team to another is possible but requires a trade cap and revenue share model where all the parties benefit. And it also requires a system where the draft and draft picks can be used as leverage to strengthen team rosters.

9. Beyond the draft: free agency and salary arbitration

Once the expansion phase concludes, there are certain components that ought to be incorporated. Auctions and drafts help establish a base from which team rosters gain a certain look and feel. Over time however, there needs to be a system in place that will allow teams to trade players' contracts, buy and sell options, and establish a system of waivers. The most crucial feature however is the concept of free agency (discussed in the paragraph below) and salary arbitration. While the latter concept can only be implemented effectively once the IPL players' association is in place, free agency—both restricted and unrestricted—must be incorporated at the earliest. The draft will still be in place for 'rookies' or 'uncapped' IPL participants each year, but beyond that, and beyond the exceptions, there is limited scope for adding talent-laden rosters to a team merely from drafts.

There are levels of free agency: restricted and unrestricted.

In restricted free agency, a player is usually free to negotiate with other teams apart from the one to which he belongs, subject to the proviso that his own team has the right of first refusal (ROFR), right of first offer (ROFO) or 'matching rights' to keep the player on board. Unrestricted free agency gives a player the right to freely negotiate and sign with any team where he feels his value is optimized. Unless the three exceptions as per the proposed IPL draft are enforced by a particular team, unrestricted free agency would give a player the option to test the market forces. He could still re-sign with his team if he so chose to, but that would be at his option and not the team's contractual right.

By IPL IV, a player draft should have been structured and implemented, since most player contracts were for three years in total with a two-year lock-in, and team option for the third year. The draft could conceivably have been implemented in time for IPL VI or latest by IPL VII. It was enough time to create a system that could stand the test of time, expansion and evolution. Simultaneously, it would have diverted attention from a toxic environment that made the gavel synonymous with auction houses, and more towards the regulated permutations and combinations that determine the draft picks. Over the long term, there should have been clearly stipulated regulations governing player trades, restricted and unrestricted free agency, a tried-and-tested formula for salary caps and floors, and proper representation for players and teams alike.

Despite its imperfections, it could have been the first step towards an enduring and sustainable system where market forces merged with passion in a hybridized league. Instead, nothing changed. The auction has continued: an embarrassing forum where legends and future stars were regularly embarrassed and ignored for no fault of their own. The allure of the auction too has waned, ironically because of the limited action over the course of a full day. In 2015, when sixty-seven players in total were picked out of a total of the 349 players entered in the auction, there is an obvious gap between the method and the result. By failing to evolve, the auction has been one of the white elephants that have defined the IPL. For an entity that was so quick to borrow concepts such as 'commissioner' and even 'league', what the IPL should really have borrowed were tried-and-tested processes, especially those that ensured quality and competitiveness. But, of course, the game had to go on, so the powers that be chose to subject the viewing public to celebrities raising boards to determine their interest in players' futures, rather than having the ability to plan and choose based on merit and not on price tags.

A draft will credit merit and remunerate the players on the basis of where they are drafted, and not because of game theory and bidding wars. Another initiative that will pay instant dividends could be borrowed from both European and North American leagues, and innovated upon. With the large rosters that each team has, many deserving players end up sidelined instead of getting a chance at glory, or missing out because of line-ups that happen to click. Teams also suffer due to unexpected injuries, player unavailability due to national duty, or limited talent available in the auction. While a preseason transfer window has been introduced with extremely limited success, one relatively easy way to improvise is by introducing two transfer and loan windows for teams to either trade players during the season with other teams, or to loan players to other teams that need to strengthen their rosters.

By introducing a mid-season loan window, and a loan window right before the play-offs, teams loaning out players will be able to offset costs and add to revenues, while teams borrowing players will be able to salvage and even bolster their seasons by filling the gaps, and mitigating the injuries or unavailability of players originally on their rosters. This will assist parity and competitiveness, along with adding a revenue vertical for teams that have spent on players but are unable to avail of their talents due to full rosters. Importantly, it will keep the fans engaged, and the players productive in a manner that is efficient and determined by market forces. A loan window right before the play-offs would make the play-offs an all-star calibre event. Imagine matches where teams can borrow the likes of David Warner, Chris Gayle or Ajinkya Rahane for the post-season matches and watch them go up against true contenders such as the MI, the KKR, and maybe someday, the CSK. So much can swing on the basis of a player selection process and a parity-driven method to ensure equality and competitiveness. The auction system has been put in place by the BCCI–IPL and followed by every other South Asian league with few exceptions. And that leaves everyone susceptible—something a league should do everything in its power to avoid. But then, is the IPL really a league? Let's find out.

6

Not a Real League

In a strictly theoretical sense, the IPL is a league. The dictionary definition of a 'league' is 'a group of teams playing a sport who take part in competitions between each other'. No one can point a finger and say the IPL is not a league in the simplest terms. But in reality, it is a league only in the simplest of terms. In most of the seasons since it began, the IPL has fielded eight teams playing fourteen matches each over a season consisting of approximately fifty-six matches (regular season) and four matches in the play-offs. In 2015, season eight of the IPL began on 8 April and concluded on 24 May. So in just about forty-six days, the IPL finished its season. Each team played seven home matches and seven away ones during the regular season, and then began the play-offs for the top four teams, with the Mumbai Indians winning their second IPL title. In league terms, this doesn't account for a very typical set-up or schedule. Across the world and especially in North America and Europe, professional sports leagues are a major part of culture and society. They extend over a significant part of the year, and involve the communities and fans of the cities in which the teams are based. Some of the more popular teams have a global following. There are seven leagues across the world that have significantly more brand awareness and higher revenues than most other leagues. In terms of financial might and recognition, North America's leagues are among the most successful—National Football League, Major League Baseball, National Basketball Association and the National Hockey League (NHL). In Europe, the most successful leagues are in football, and rival the North American leagues when it comes to global popularity and revenues. The two most popular of these are the English Premier League and Spain's La Liga. While these are by no means the only successful leagues in Europe, they have a stronger market presence and brand value than other popular football leagues in the region, such as the German Bundesliga or Italy's Serie A.

An apples-to-apples comparison between the IPL and the world's most successful and popular leagues will be somewhat difficult given the unique nature of cricket's disproportionately skewed emphasis on international fixtures, as compared to more traditional leagues that have a much larger window to schedule their matches/games, and where the club component has equal weightage to national duty. North American leagues, in fact, have an almost completely skewed emphasis on club competition where the league duties replace any obligation on players to participate in international fixtures for their respective countries. American football, baseball, ice hockey and basketball have limited international fixtures, so the league takes precedence. For football, the clubs versus country obligations are quite clearly set out, and obligations are for qualification matches for players representing their home countries, either for World Cup qualifiers or, for Europeans, the Euro qualifiers.

The evolution of the IPL is, of course, unique when compared to any other professional sports league in the world. Unlike North American professional sports leagues, cricket is dominated by the international calendar, and cannot emulate their processes. Football leagues, including the EPL, have a system that takes into account the international calendar, but they do have players available to them for the bulk of each season. The player selection process in the EPL involves loans, purchases and trades, but the system is evolved to the extent that there is a methodology and framework whereby the selling team, the purchasing team, the league, and the player concerned—all benefit from the transaction.

Due to a loaded international calendar, the IPL, for the most part, is the shortest league in terms of duration and overall time commitment. It also enjoys the enviable situation whereby the world's best cricketers and overall cricket talent pool, with very few exceptions, are usually available for selection. What it doesn't have yet, however, is a player selection, retention and transfer process that is sophisticated, dynamic or robust enough to keep pace with the rapidly evolving (and escalating) pay scales and related requirements to ensure parity and equitable distribution. But that's a different story altogether.

Currently, the IPL is not really in a position to compete with any of the leading sports leagues of the world in actual terms, but amazingly its popularity keeps it competitive in various statistics. This could be temporary and attributable to the lack of real competition in its sport (although this is changing), the barrier to entry that the IPL has, and above all else, the captive fan base of South Asia and pockets of Europe, North America and Asia, among others.

Let's look at the three most well-known and successful professional sports leagues in the world as independent models, and then compare their salient aspects to the IPL to draw parallels and contrasts. The three leagues we can look at are: a) the EPL which is widely considered the most watched and popular sports league in the world; b) the NFL which has a similar number of games per team to the IPL but a completely different operating system and asset accumulation structure; and c) MLB which happens to be the lengthiest league in terms of number of games that each team plays per season.

Let's set some baseline facts in place for what most leagues internationally possess as a norm and then look at each league in turn:

a. All three leagues we will be looking at have an established system of asset and revenue accumulation, with owners of the teams also having representation at the level of the central council. So owners are decision-makers in each league, not merely recipients and implementers of instructions. Each of the three leagues has a system in place whereby the teams have ownership of, or a long-term stake in, home stadiums. This gives them an asset that independently gives value to the team. Alongside the home stadium asset is the support that teams get from the city/state/province governments, local authorities, municipalities and others. The cities frequently are involved with the incubation, functioning and success of the teams which bear the cities' names.

b. Teams within the leagues through the interplay with the people of their cities have built a strong ground-level loyalty base, which leads to extensive and consistent gate revenues through corporate boxes, season tickets, overall support, and merchandise sales in addition to a share of central revenues that teams receive based on performance and equity in the league.

c. Related to point b is the length of the season each year, which allows fans to develop familiarity with players and team branding, as well as a fierce sense of city and team loyalty.

d. Ownership of the leagues is invariably private, that is, the national federation in each country where the league operates is not directly involved with the ownership or operations of the league. Rather they are only sanctioning bodies granting the leagues 'official' status, although for baseball and American football, there isn't really a global governing body with influence, since neither is an Olympic sport in the true sense. The EPL does have the sanction of England's Football Association (FA) but the FA does not have equity in or direct involvement with the running of the EPL.

e. Talent development and a farming system are consistent across almost every mature league in the world. This can be in the form of a direct feeder system such as the one that the NFL and the MLB have through a complex, extensive and successful collegiate system—the National Collegiate Athletic Association, the umbrella organization for all college and university sports. Or, it could be in the form of development teams/training squads such as the ones that the EPL, La Liga, NFL and MLB have, where players are tried out and then gradually elevated to the major league squad—a lengthy learning and proving time. Talent spotting, developing, and a gruelling minor league or development farming system are consistent in all mature leagues in sophisticated sports jurisdictions. It is a necessary component for ensuring quality, depth and replenishment of superstars which make the leagues successful.

f. Linked to performance and quality sustainability is a mechanism in each successful league that incentivizes good performance and punishes consistently poor performance season after season. Most of it is a financial check and balance, when successful seasons are rewarded by full stadiums, merchandise sales, a larger share of profits from the central league, and an enhanced brand value. In leagues where the relegations system is used, a successful season in the second tier is rewarded by a promotion to the top tier which automatically results in exponentially higher revenues. In conference-based leagues, poor performances aren't directly punished but there are enough disincentives and also incentives to succeed such as lottery picks in drafts and the opportunity to rebuild teams, as earlier explained in Chapter 5. Unsuccessful seasons are punished by lower profitability across verticals, a shorter season due to not making the play-offs, and in relegation-based leagues, a relegation to the second tier which means a huge reduction in revenues, exposure and profitability.

g. A unique feature of North American leagues is the collective bargaining arrangement whereby the players are represented by a players' union and aided by professionals to negotiate in bulk the wages, rights and other crucial components of the league with the owners and the office of the commissioner.

h. Lastly, whether developed over time or modified due to scandal, most successful leagues have a detailed, extensive, diligent and process-driven method to ownership or ownership changes. Yes, there are many flamboyant owners in many of the leagues but their antecedents are almost always in the public domain, and they undergo scrutiny and the Know Your Investor process before being given the ownership reins of teams.

With the above components in mind, let's look at the three leagues I have shortlisted.

The EPL is the one league which has a global following, a passionate fan base, and is instantly recognizable even in a cricket-crazy country like India. It has natural advantages of history, the popularity of football globally, a location in the most central time zone and geographical placement for television viewership, and a brand that is virtually unparalleled. England also has perhaps the deepest, most comprehensive and exhaustive development system for amateur and professional football in the world.[1] Let's look at the numbers: there are at least 346 teams that play competitive football in the UK. Ninety-two teams play formal league football parallel to each other. The EPL features twenty teams, each playing thirty-eight games over a season that extends over eight months, from August to May. There are 380 games played each season, and a majority of the stadiums are sold out for the entire season. It follows a promotion and relegation system where each season, the three of the worst-performing teams are relegated to the second-tier football league, and three of the best-performing teams from the second tier are promoted to the EPL. The EPL isn't the oldest sports league in the world, far from it; it, in fact, is relatively young, and its current format has only been in existence since 1992. But the EPL has over 125 years of league football precedents that have contributed to its current structure and popularity, with the erstwhile top-tier and current second-tier football league being the oldest such league in the world, founded in 1888. The EPL is structured as a limited company and is independent of the football association of England. It therefore operates as a private corporation with a CEO, board of directors and other key personnel who ensure that the league is operated professionally. It also allows the league to follow governance and diligence norms along the lines of well-run corporations that look at the bottom line and how to attain it ethically. Each of the twenty teams is a shareholder and therefore part-owner of the EPL. Two of the biggest revenue streams in the EPL, besides broadcast rights, are stadium-related revenues (gate receipts and in-stadia naming rights/signage), and sales of merchandise. Each of the teams also has a major physical asset that contributes to its valuation and net worth: its stadium. By owning the stadium, each team not only is able to sell all associated branding and stadium rights (a lucrative business), but it also has a tangible physical asset that can be leveraged and isn't merely speculative or dependent on league and industry goodwill. Ownership of the stadiums also allows them the right to receive sponsorship monies for naming rights, for example, the Emirates Stadium for Arsenal, or the Etihad Stadium for Manchester City.

Player acquisitions and transfers happen under the centralized FIFA rules on the status and transfer of players, and these are consistent for football leagues anywhere in the world. So there really isn't room for loopholes in terms of player retentions or squads theoretically. Teams have development systems that nurture talent, either for their own competitive purposes, or to trade to other clubs and thereby add a revenue source for player trades, sales or loans.

Merchandising is also a significant source of revenue for EPL teams, but the biggest source of revenue for the EPL is through broadcast rights. For the 2016–19 period, the domestic broadcast rights totalled £5.136 billion, which was a 71 per cent increase over the previous broadcast rights package.[2] It is deals such as these that ensure the success of the EPL teams. Four of the teams in the EPL are valued at over one billion USD each. It is, of course, easier to value the EPL teams since virtually every team owns a prime piece of real estate/physical asset in the form of a stadium, a real physical asset that it can mortgage or borrow against. There is international ownership spread across the EPL, and in terms of owner diversity, the EPL has perhaps the most diverse owner group among any sports league in the world. The most successful clubs—Manchester United and Arsenal, Manchester City and Chelsea have US, UAE and Russian majority owners respectively.

Major League Baseball, or the MLB, is one of North America's favourite pastimes. Although there are not less than seven mature professional sports leagues in the US, baseball and American football have a special place in American hearts. Of the two, baseball and, in fact, the MLB is the most analogous to cricket in India. So analogous that there was even a recent initiative to recruit two Indians to the MLB as pitchers, which then led to the Disney full-length feature *Million Dollar Arm*. In terms of game duration, basic features of throwing, catching, and hitting, the two are intuitively similar, although there are many differences in actuality. One of the oldest sports and leagues of North America, the MLB has been in existence since 1903, and is an integral part of North American culture.[3] The MLB season is extremely long, with each team playing a staggering 162 games, not including the play-offs, which for a World Series–winning team, could be another 12–19 games more. The MLB features thirty teams in total divided into two separate leagues and then further divided into divisions. It was the MLB which had the Black Sox scandal; it was baseball which first integrated the race issue during the civil rights movements in the

US, and it is baseball which frequently faces disciplinary hearings and ethics breakdowns. Doping in the MLB has been a major issue, as has been the lack of competitiveness for small-market teams versus large-market teams such as the New York Yankees or the Los Angeles Dodgers. The MLB does not have a salary cap, so team owners can spend as much as they like on acquiring players, and payrolls often exceed US$100–200 million annually. Given the number of games played and the length of the season, merchandising and season tickets are major contributors to a team's revenues. The MLB has also aggressively tackled many of the governance breakdowns, due in part to a shake-up from the political section, when during the doping scandals certain players were forced to testify before a grand jury, at congressional hearings[4] and then were prosecuted for perjury. The image of the MLB is still not completely rectified, but baseball has always received elite treatment from the judiciary and the lawmakers in the US. One of the oldest anti-trust judgments in the US pertained to interstate commerce which was a contentious point between states in the late 1800s. Baseball was found to be exempt from the limitations of interstate commerce, and in a 1922 Supreme Court ruling, it was exempted from anti-trust laws. The MLB in its current structure has existed from 2000 onward, and is led by the office of the commissioner, a title we may all be familiar with. Like all the other mature sports leagues, the MLB is professionally run, with upper-management personnel handling the MLB's affairs, along with its sister concern that handles the media. The MLB is one of the most watched leagues in large part due to the length of the season. It has one of the deepest and most rigorous farming systems known as the 'minor leagues'. Minor league teams are attached to the major league clubs, and call-ups for players who are performing well in the minor leagues to the major leagues, as well as demotions for major league players to the minor leagues occur through the season. It is this farming system that keeps the talent consistent and allows teams to perform at full strength even if injuries occur to key players. It also keeps the sport alive and visible in smaller towns where the minor league teams are located, and which don't have major league teams playing in the vicinity. There are 240 minor league teams that fall under the purview of the commissioner of the MLB.

Stadium ownership in the MLB and the NFL varies from team to team. Given that seasons can be scheduled based on stadium availability, there are many cities which have both an MLB and an NFL team, and which have built multi-purpose stadiums to allow both city teams to play home games there. The MLB has quite a few lessons that can be imparted to the IPL, although in terms of seasons and the components that go into a season, the two are like chalk and cheese. Perhaps the single most powerful professional sports league in the world is the NFL. By virtue of value, popularity, commercials and the single biggest sporting event across the world, the Super Bowl, the NFL leads every parameter used to gauge success. In North America, American football has three main components to every season: high school football on Friday nights, college football on Saturdays, and the NFL games on Sunday, and one game on Monday night each week with occasional games on Thursdays as well. The NFL features thirty-two teams in a seventeen-week season, commencing in the first week of September and concluding in the last week of December, following which the play-offs begin. Each team plays sixteen games in the regular season which determines qualification for the play-offs. There are 256 games played each season, and the NFL has the highest average attendance of any league in the world, which in large part is due to the size of the stadiums each team play their games in. Although in existence since 1920, the current version of the NFL has been in place since 1966 and the Super Bowl began that year. Until recently, the NFL was a not-for-profit set-up, but that is no longer the case starting 2015. The NFL now is a set-up which is owned and financed by the thirty-two team owners on whose behalf a commissioner, treasurer and secretary operate the league. The commissioner in the NFL has broad powers, including the right to negotiate disputes, suspend players, terminate franchises for due cause, and ban players for life if they are suspected of fixing games or illegally betting. The NFL is a team-first structure where revenues and value emanate from the individual teams, thereby creating a holistic league system. Today, the NFL is the most successful professional sports league in the world, by virtue of value, revenue and the success of its teams. It is also the most balanced when it comes to net worth.

To elucidate the current positioning of teams in terms of value, according to the *Forbes* list of top professional sports teams for 2015, twenty of the top fifty sports franchises in the world based on value belonged to the NFL. The highest-ranked NFL team is Dallas Cowboys, which is at the number two spot with a value of US$3.2 billion. The MLB has twelve teams in the top fifty, with New York Yankees in a tie for the second place with Cowboys. The EPL has four teams out of the top fifty, with Manchester United the highest at fifth place with a value of US$3.1 billion. The other three EPL teams in the top fifty are Manchester City at twenty-ninth place with US$1.39 billion, Chelsea at thirty-first position valued at US$1.37 billion, and Arsenal at thirty-sixth position with a value of US$1.31 billion. Football has a solid presence in the top ten overall, with La Liga's two flagship teams leading from the front. La Liga is seen as a top-heavy league, and the numbers reflect that as well, with Real Madrid topping the list for a third consecutive year with a value of US$3.26 billion, and Barcelona FC at fourth place with a value of US$3.16 billion. The Bundesliga has just one team in the top fifty, with Bayern Munich, considered one of the most appealing clubs globally, occupying the eleventh place with a value of US$2.35 billion.[5] It goes without saying that there is quite a gap between the IPL teams and successful teams in mature leagues in terms of branding and value. Although there is no official report on the most successful or highest-earning sports leagues of the world, based on revenues and value of each league, in terms of annual revenue and revenue per club, the top seven leagues are: the NFL, MLB, EPL, NBA, NHL, La Liga and the Bundesliga. The IPL is far behind the leading North American and European leagues, and that is not only expected but also understandable. The IPL, as it currently stands, falls somewhere between the thirty-fifth and forty-fifth positions among leagues in the world. Which, given how young it is, and how most of Europe and Asia, and almost all of North America don't really play or follow cricket, is quite an impressive feat. But given the sky-high expectations that the IPL propagates, there is a long way to go before it figures in discussions about the most successful leagues in the world. In all honesty, given the limitations it faces, and the difficulty in altering or increasing the current structure, the IPL may never reach the levels of the EPL, the NFL or the MLB. If it does make some positive changes however, it will definitely increase the likelihood of success. Until now, the changes have not been ones meant with intent, and have focused instead on instant gratification and overnight results. Every other league in its history has, at some point, faced a dissolution of the existing set-up, or have grown with a merger with a competitor or split from the parent association and become private, professionally run bodies. The IPL too would likely face similar evolutionary changes during its life cycle. The BCCI needs to be prepared to handle adversity, and to be flexible in its handling of setbacks, because there will be plenty more going forward, even if the board really does a volte-face and works towards cleaning up the entire sport.

The IPL follows no real precedent of international sports leagues. There are justifiable reasons for this—firstly, the international calendar and the ICC's reluctance to grant the IPL a place in the schedule mean that there is only the short window of forty-five to sixty days in a year for the IPL to be held, and even within that window, there are international fixtures for countries other than India. Secondly, resources for creating infrastructure are lacking, and a window as short as the IPL's may not be cost-effective in terms of building a stadium. For the time being, other sports leagues are too small or not lucrative enough to consider sharing the cost of a multisport stadium. Also, by building a private stadium, the board risks angering the relevant state associations who would see a significant decline in the revenues that they receive for the temporary leasing out of the home stadia to the IPL franchises. Lastly, the IPL follows a different set of rules than almost any other league in the world, simply because for the time being, it can. It has seen comparisons to the world's best and biggest leagues in a matter of just a couple of years, which is unprecedented. For some time at least, the IPL's position is relatively safe but the growth and comparisons have plateaued and stalled respectively. Nomenclatures have been borrowed, but not processes, and because the IPL doesn't operate as a typical or traditional league, it faces many challenges to its overall well-being. This is the biggest downside to its growth and its contribution to Indian cricket.

The IPL doesn't follow the system used in football leagues for relegation wherein a two- to three-tier league structure automatically rewards improvement in performance. It also doesn't follow the North American league system of minor leagues and farming talent. The latter, based on which the IPL was set up, would be particularly helpful for improving the quality of domestic T20 cricket, and also to help the BCCI serve its primary role of developing cricket at all levels. Even if the BCCI spins off the IPL into a separate private entity like I have recommended it to do, the farming system is one which would be easy to accomplish—it would bring T20 cricket to the smaller towns and stadiums, would help imbibe a culture of season-long or even year-long domestic T20 competition, and help

India establish itself as the best development model for churning out elite talent. Why the BCCI hasn't done this yet is puzzling, because it's really quite simple. Restrict it to the domestic players, and if availability is the problem, restrict it initially to the uncapped players contracted to each franchise. For the initial season or two, the minor league can operate roughly for the duration of the IPL— it doesn't have to be restricted to that window, but just initially. Each player who is not in the playing eleven or final fifteen for his franchise will be a part of the minor league. He will participate in the minor league throughout the season, and if for any reason he is required to play for his franchise in the IPL, he can be called up and available literally within hours. If he is performing exceptionally at the minor leagues, his franchise can call him up and send an underperforming replacement down to get practice and regain form.

Money to organize this is not a problem—not only is the IPL cash-rich, it is the BCCI's obligation and responsibility to develop and promote the sport of cricket. Availability of players too is not a good enough reason. The BCCI controls cricket—if it genuinely wants to improve and ensure the quality of Indian talent, it must have a second-tier league as a proving ground. It is something the IPL would greatly benefit from, even if it isn't commercially lucrative. At some point, the demarcation must be made, and a minor league is a must-have for the BCCI–IPL.

The relegation system will be a much more challenging system to adopt for the IPL. Primarily, and unfortunately due to the fact that it has been unable to even field eight teams consistently and without drama, to expect it to have a roster of twenty to twenty-five teams playing across tiers for the right to remain in the main IPL is unrealistic. The IPL, due to its brevity, its inability to provide tangible revenue sources to its franchises, and its fame-first outlook towards ownership of teams, will be unable to successfully replicate the EPL or La Liga model for T20 cricket.

Another big void is the absence of a players' representative body, an offshoot of the board's reluctance to allow for such an organization for the contracted players in the national squad. The lack of representation can work at the national level even though it's not ideal, because there are limited negotiation points or obligations that the players must meet, barring intuitive basic dos and don'ts. The IPL is much more complex and complicated when it comes to a player's responsibilities, rights, and failures. Especially for uncapped players of Indian origin who would in all likelihood have never seen a contract or a detailed code of conduct that the IPL governing council expects them to understand and follow. The spot-fixing controversy was one such failure, as was the Jadeja suspension. The IPL giving the players a voice and allowing them a centralized pool of professionals to help guide them, mentor them and protect them will be doing a great service. Especially to the upcoming youngsters who won't then have to grapple with integrity dilemmas on their own. Equally importantly, they won't have to feel the need to trust someone blindly for lack of options, and thus risk being misled. Now, with the Justice Lodha Committee recommending a players' representative body for cricketers overall, perhaps a subset for the IPL players too should be looked at seriously.

The IPL's main competitor today in India is a professional football league that was conceptualized by the IMG-Reliance joint venture and Star India Pvt. Ltd—the Hero Indian Super League. Learning from the mistakes that the IPL's management regularly and consistently made, the ISL, in just its second season is already a moderate success. More importantly, it has set out at least a few crucial governance parameters that ought to make the IPL governing council sit up and take notice.

Ownership criterion is strict and unbending as is the paper trail disclosure requirement. The requirement of year-round activity in the development of football is another solid move. The relationship with the All India Football Federation (AIFF) is at arm's length, so the first degree of conflict of interest has been taken care of. Of course, mistakes that generate interest have also been repeated in the ISL, such as the player auction, although the ISL has introduced a hybrid version featuring both an auction as well as a draft for those players not selected through the auction process.[6] The revenue model is at least for now uncertain and the broadcast rights are intrinsically allocated to Star India; so one major chunk of potential revenue does not accrue on market dynamics to the franchises. That is however offset by the massive promotional campaign and deep-rooted broadcast of the ISL in regional languages and across its vast network. So although there isn't a clear-cut broadcast rights revenue share, the promotion and branding of the league ought to have a positive, direct and pecuniary benefit to the franchise owners and the league. Also, and this is again a factor of scheduling like the IPL, the ISL's schedule is short for a league. Therefore, revenues and asset building may be compromised in the interest of an entertaining but not very meaningful sports league.

There is a possibility of the ISL becoming the sole football league in India, in which case it may have to merge with the AIFF-run I-League, or replace it. Discussions are under way. But in the current scenario, although the ISL is competitive with the IPL, it doesn't have the strength to topple the IPL's position of power. Football is not India's strength, and despite pockets of India being passionate about football, India's position in world football is dismal both on-field and off-field. The football leagues across the world are formidable, and the best players are contracted to them. Unlike the IPL and the BCCI's stature in world cricket, the ISL will take a long time before it can promise world-class football action featuring some of the premier footballers of the world. And unlike in cricket, a league dependent on the Indian players in football is not a winning proposition. For the time being at least, the IPL has space between itself and the next competitor in South Asia.

What the IPL has done better than any other league in the world is merge the worlds of entertainment and sport, and simply submerge the population with marketing and advertising blasts that make the IPL impossible to ignore. The involvement of celebrities as sweat-equity holders in franchises or even as active majority owners has been a masterstroke for publicity and immersion with Indian society. It showed a shrewd understanding by Modi of how important Bollywood was to the success of the IPL or any sports property for that matter. With almost no exception, every Bollywood personality has a role or purpose in the IPL—entrenched or superficial. It's a model that now every sports league in India is following, and the ISL has followed it extremely successfully, apparently making it a prerequisite for franchises to have someone with star power in their stakeholder roles.

The difference between the IPL and the world's top professional sports leagues is in terms of age/maturity, professionalism, asset and revenue verticals, positioning and also global exposure. For it to be taken seriously and to not fall prey to competition, stagnation, opposition or indefinite suspension, it will need to tailor itself to meet the requirements demanded of professional sports leagues. It's a good thing, not a negative that the IPL has been so very successful despite the limited offerings. It will be even better if the IPL adjusts, accommodates, adds and implements basic frameworks, verticals and compliances beyond those it already has. It will be good for perception, better self-protection/insurance against unsavoury developments, and great for the viewing public and players—the two most valuable commodities that the IPL and the board must look after. A lack of transparency or perceived governance lapses will also hurt the value of the league and teams since listed companies who traditionally sponsor events, leagues or sportspersons do care about the association and stigma being passed on to them. The FIFA scandal is one such example, the Lance Armstrong debacle is another. Good governance will help the IPL generate more value for itself.

7

The IPL's Future: Sink or Swim

The board and the IPL enter the next phase in an extremely unfamiliar spot—that of an underdog. The BCCI–IPL is trying to solve the many puzzles and disruptions it has faced recently. The IPL is not the first sports league to face extreme controversy and challenges to its existence; it also won't be the last. Perhaps it's unique in that so much has happened to it in its first few years of operations that it feels as if it's constantly battling one crisis after another. It is one of the few entities across industries, verticals or continents where its entire success or sustainability depends entirely on its own actions. Its own behaviour or laxity leading to omissions is what causes most of its headaches, and now, of course, there is external watchdogging happening at the highest echelons of justice. And despite everything, including the many criticisms of it and its owner/promoter—the board's handling of it—the IPL's future remains bright, and it controls its own destiny. As things stand, the IPL may not have reached the lofty heights predicted of it in 2008 and then 2010, but it remains immensely successful.

In terms of TRPs, IPL 2015 actually increased its reach from IPL 2014, and attracted approximately 192 million viewers.[1] Despite the overhaul in sponsorships and the changing of guard as sponsors, at no point have the league or the franchises not had options, almost instantaneously. Live audiences at the stadiums remain consistent even if not outstanding.

The challenges to the IPL are self-imposed. All of that can be revised, and none of it actually takes away from the future success of the event. First of all, yes, the IPL has been plagued by scandal and controversy throughout its existence. And yes, there appear to have been umpteen governance lapses both at the central and team levels. But the truth is that every sports league in the history of professional sports has faced similar scandals at certain points in time. How the league or individual teams emerge from the controversies they face determines their destiny and legacy.

There are many things the IPL did correctly, right from the start. It had and in many respects still has the blueprint for creating an extremely successful sports event in India. They say imitation is the best possible flattery, and the IPL has been mimicked in India in every shape, size, form and sport. There is virtually no sport in India today that hasn't had a 'league' model that imitates the IPL almost to the core. It goes to show the landscape change that the IPL brought to sports in India. It wasn't the first league in India—it's merely the most well-known and in comparative terms, the most successful. It often doesn't get the credit it deserves. When one reads or hears about the IPL, it is almost always described as a 'cash-rich league'. I doubt if anyone has ever stopped and wondered why this is, and whether it's a good thing for a league or tournament to be cash-rich.

Yes, in many ways the IPL is cash-rich, at least for the central league and for the board. Just by virtue of being the dominant cricket body of the world, the BCCI has a distinct advantage that it passes on to the IPL. Through sponsorships and franchise fees, the IPL at the holistic and central level is a cash-making juggernaut. There are few costs it has to bear with the exception of management at the strategic level, and affiliated expenses. Perhaps marketing and promotion is another cost head but much of that is covered by the broadcaster, the sponsors leveraging their association and the franchises trying to get fans to become a part of the frenzy. The IPL is cash-rich in large part because it simply does not reinvest its 'cash' to make the revenue verticals for all those vested in the league to eventually make profit. The cricket is often exciting, and many of the owners and their guests are frequently enthused, but in terms of building upon all the natural advantages that the IPL has had, its innovativeness for new business ideas to enlarge the revenue pie has been uninspiring. This to a large degree is why we don't see a whole lot of change in each successive IPL season. Perhaps it's complacency or perhaps it's restrictiveness given the limited time frame and freedom the BCCI–IPL has.

The recipe for the IPL's success was intuitive and intrinsic. It was destined to do well and the recipe was ingenious at the time. In a seller's market, the IPL was the perfect product to pitch and captivate. Perhaps it did everything in too much of a hurry and with not enough diligence, and then the trouble began. The trouble though is only as much as the BCCI lets it be. Through internal clashes, questionable overlap of commercial interest, and a fiercely private mindset, the veil of impregnability dissipated, and when it rained it poured. It was hampered by the spot-fixing scandal and then the scandal became a huge controversy.

Taken individually, each of the issues could easily have been handled at the time, and to be fair to the board and the IPL governing council, quite a few of the issues were unavoidable even if the governance mechanism had been flawless. There was an unfortunate fight to retain control of the board in a clear conflict of interest situation, and things just spiralled. The court felt the board was either unwilling or unable to fix the problem, and it stepped in by empowering two independent and neutral committees to analyse and reprimand the offenders. The reprimand went further than any other action in history taken against cricket in India, and it is still ongoing. In a nutshell, that brings us up to speed to October 2015. Here's the funny thing—even today when one questions if the IPL can even survive or sustain itself, the answer is simple. Of course, it can. It has defied logic by generating revenue beyond its apparent offerings, and the demand for association with the IPL is still significant. Even if today it puts its books in order, overhauls the governance lapses in anti-corruption, buyer due diligence and nipping the conflict of interest, the IPL will thunder ahead like an incredible machine. Yes, it has dropped a couple of sitters in terms of prior warnings through franchise controversies or warnings by the court, but now it has been given a difficult half-chance, and this is one ball it cannot afford to drop. It's a must-take and if it now cleans up with positive intent all that it is accused of, no one will stand in its way.

Whatever the reason for the IPL's hurting image, it's unfortunate because it, for all its recent setbacks, scandals and fiscal shocks, has changed the young Indian's perspective, and has been a cultural opinion maker. It has put India on the map of sports, and it has attracted some of the best human capital to work in an environment exclusively built to entertain Indian society. Even Bollywood has bowed to the IPL's might, limiting new releases during the IPL seasons. Whatever the question marks are regarding the league, people still watch it. And sponsors still buy into the brand. On 27 October 2015, the board announced Vivo as the third title sponsor of the IPL since it first began. Vivo took over from Pepsico which withdrew in 2015, and according to Anurag Thakur, Vivo was not the only party interested in taking on the title sponsorship. So the BCCI–IPL has two relatively less-known entities sponsoring its two prime properties—the Indian team now sponsored by PayTM replacing Star India which didn't extend its contract on lapsing, and Vivo replacing Pepsi midway through the term as IPL's title sponsor. It's indicative of brands leveraging cricket and the IPL to announce their presence, meaning despite all the setbacks, the IPL still catches more eyeballs than any other sports or entertainment property in India.[2] I had mentioned earlier how the reverse bidding process for the two interim franchises turned out to be a victory for the board. Nothing speaks more to the value and positioning of brand IPL than the recent reverse bidding process used to decide which entities would get a chance to operate a franchise in the IPL for two years as replacements for the suspended Chennai and Rajasthan teams. The very fact that each entity was willing to invest the kind of money it committed for a short-term association means that the reputation or brand hit aside, the IPL remains the strongest and most coveted sponsor or investor association in Indian sports. Earlier, I had also mentioned the concerns the IPL would have in the future with regard to competition from other T20 leagues. Also interesting is that the player allocation methodology for the two interim franchises is through a draft rather than the auction, where five players each from the suspended Chennai and Rajasthan teams will be allocated to the two franchises. Perhaps finally the board is seeing the merit of substance over shock value when it comes to player allocations. One can always hope.

Speaking of player drafts, the newly launched PSL has chosen a draft system rather than an auction for its player allocation. So here's a potentially strong competitor by way of the PSL, a twenty-five-day event to be held annually in the United Arab Emirates, featuring players from Pakistan and the rest of the world, except for India. Given the success and popularity of Pakistan's players, especially in T20 cricket, and given that the Pakistan players don't or can't participate in the IPL, this apples-and-oranges match-up could have been an indicator of where the IPL stood as a professional T20 league. In round one, the IPL emphatically dismissed the challenge. The PSL in its franchisee auction could only generate US$93 million for the five teams combined, the broadcasting deal is in the vicinity of US$ 15 million, and the sponsorships are said to be in the US$ 6 million range.[3] Contrast this with the IPL where just the central revenue contribution to each franchise is expected to be in the US$11–13 million (or INR 70–75 crores) range annually.[4] This means the IPL is the ultimate big brother of T20 cricket across the world, but at the same time, the IPL must be careful it doesn't overstep the line of propriety, because there are many big brothers watching over it back home in India.

Back in 2009 if the BCCI had been a more compassionate establishment and if the IPL had been a less jarring and more associable property, many, if not all of us, would have been proud of it. As Indians, to have the IPL belong to us and showcase the best in the world at our home stadiums was a luxury that was forgotten due to the various sideshows and the tarnish that lay just below the surface of the league's shimmering persona.

The IPL has successfully popularized T20 cricket across the world, and has been the first to commercialize sports in India. It accomplished in less than a year what other leagues took half a century or more to do. The blueprint was ingenious in its making and even today keeps it not only afloat, but also a part and parcel of urban culture. If it can turn things around and overcome adversity, tweak some glaring flaws, eradicate integrity lapses, and invest in a sustainable future, the IPL is still a formidable force. It isn't that hard to get it right. And, with the court willing to play a support function to enable implementation of safety nets and seamless transparency, the IPL is in pole position to make it all happen for the positive. It has to remember to sell the sport, veer away from shock, and gravitate to substance.

To make the biggest impact, the IPL should be privatized and it should be established along the lines of best practices, not a hybrid of good practices and uncertain modifications. As I had touched upon briefly in earlier sections, on 4 October 2015, the person whom many feel could be the candidate of change took the reins in his second term as BCCI president. For many who felt that things were beginning to go from bad to worse, Shashank Manohar's return to the BCCI was one of the first really positive moves for Indian cricket. A vocal critic of many of the IPL's omissions, his unopposed election ushered in the post-Srinivasan era for the BCCI–IPL. For Manohar, this is legacy-building time, and he has every opportunity to highlight the distinction between him and Srinivasan, and change the course of the BCCI's downward spiral in recent years. He started strongly. Within just a couple of months of taking over the BCCI, he made a number of positive moves culminating in the AGM where control measures for conflict of interest were instituted. More importantly, he professed both the intent and the action steps towards cleaner and more level-headed governance measures. By replacing Srinivasan as the chairman of the ICC, he is likely to unify more support amongst the possibly disgruntled boards unhappy with the balance of power of the Big Three. When asked about the current world order of cricket, Manohar didn't mince his words: 'I don't agree with the three major countries bullying the ICC . . . that's my personal view, because as I have always said, an institution is bigger than individuals.'[5]

Manohar is considered to be one of the cleanest in terms of reputation for ethical behaviour in the BCCI, and at this juncture 'clean' is the choicest plaudit a cricket administrator can hope to have. He comes at a time when the board has been making moves towards redemption albeit with trepidation. That should change, basis his statement immediately upon taking charge. Asking for a period of two months to begin the turnaround, he spoke with intent and appeared to have a strong game plan for positive change. His timing is good, and perhaps his tenure will be the board's last definitive chance to make amends for decades of complacency and opaqueness, and also rescue the IPL. He may not even get a full term to change things around; the need for positive moves is that urgent a priority. One of his supporters is the current BCCI secretary, Anurag Thakur, who in the interim led the board towards what were positive moves made by it to clot the ebbing goodwill of Indian cricket. There are many downsides to having public officials serve dual roles, and I had set those out in the earlier section on conflict of interest. Manohar too has not addressed the duality of roles for politicians/government officials and whether they will be regulated or barred from involvement with the BCCI–IPL till such time they are detached from the public role. It will take time to ensure the transition from dual roles to dedicated professionals and administrators turning things around for cricket. With that in mind, it does appear that for the present situation, Thakur has made some solid moves towards fixing what has been wrong, and with Manohar, they seem to have a comfort and common resolve. For that, he and other like-minded officials in the BCCI deserve some credit.

Manohar must judiciously and firmly steer the BCCI towards transparency, and rein in the IPL before the

Supreme Court steps in and does it for him and the board. For Manohar, helping the BCCI improve its image, and stepping in to fix the failures of the IPL should not only be a priority, but should come naturally. In his first couple of days back at the helm, Manohar announced some progressive priorities—creating an ombudsman for ethics and governance, cracking down on state cricket associations by holding them accountable for funds received, and putting the BCCI constitutional documents online. This indicates a realization that platitudes are passé, and that if the board doesn't do it, the court might just.

Manohar has the opportunity to make his tenure count. He has been elected unopposed, so he has the support of the entire board. He has come at a time when reform is no longer just an option, and with the tacit approval of the court for making far-reaching changes to the board and the IPL, he doesn't even need to put himself out on a limb or walk the plank over proactive reform. Given his distance from personal commercial interests from cricket, making profit from the IPL or causing conflict to his own interest won't be real concerns. With the proverbial two birds and one stone equation he can smite and cauterize the Srinivasan era, and rectify one of the biggest failures of the BCCI and IPL by coming down hard on any conflict of interest of any nature in Indian cricket. He should start by fixing the biggest conflict of interest in cricket today—the BCCI owning the IPL.

The regime disappointed in the working group meeting on 18 October 2015 when it didn't take a hard stance on the eight-versus-ten team dilemma it faces in the IPL, but all its other moves were positive. The working group appointed the consulting firm Deloitte to assess and oversee a variety of governance and integrity issues and to implement solutions that enhanced good governance. The key areas included monitoring the usage of funds given to state associations, ordering commentators to be contracted only to the broadcaster and not to the board, and putting the board's elusive constitution online. The mandate for Deloitte, within the aptly titled Project Transformation, should be path-breaking as it adopts tracking, accountability and up-to-date processes for financial transactions within its scope.[6] During the meeting, Manohar unveiled a series of planned moves to eradicate conflict of interest across all levels, leaving no one exempt to pursue a dual role. This was excellent news. Some of the suggested changes were: (a) ensuring that administrators, officials, players, ex-players, and near relatives of any of the aforementioned would neither have commercial interest in cricket, nor dual roles, nor positions that would trigger conflicts of interest; (b) installing an ethics ombudsman who would hear grievances pertaining to conflict of interest, and opine within thirty days of the hearing; (c) implementing the player–agent accreditation requirement to ensure that unethical relationships don't form; (d) precluding administrators and their near relatives from being on the payrolls of IPL franchises, with the same restrictions for administrators and their near relatives, preventing them from being associated with companies/organizations that have entered commercial agreements with the BCCI–IPL; (e) precluding BCCI officials and their near relatives from being involved with player management companies; (f) parallel bars on state associations, their administrators and officials from having similar relationships or arrangements at the state level; (g) preventing conflict of interest for team selectors and personnel and their near relatives by barring them from having a financial arrangement or business interest with any player on the squad; (h) a bar on players having business associations or financial arrangements with other players in the squad; (i) a bar on cricketers holding contracts with the BCCI from having any other role in a BCCI committee or the IPL governing council; (j) making retirement from all forms of cricket a requirement for consideration as a coach or selector of the BCCI; (k) preventing coaches and selectors from having private commercial interests in cricket, including a bar on running private academies, being associated with player management companies, and association with media houses for writing, etc.; (l) amending the BCCI's constitution to eliminate the president's veto right in cricketing affairs— in the past it had been used controversially by presidents, including by Srinivasan; and (m) recommending three external members for the IPL governing council, who should be individuals with impeccable credentials, integrity and experience in finance and administration. Many of the suggestions were ahead of, yet consistent with, the Justice Lodha Committee's recommendations of January 2016. However, the implementation of most of the suggestions has been anything but rapid.

The board's annual general meeting took place on 9 November 2015, and quite a few of the initial suggestions made by Manohar were implemented, although some weren't. Dealing with conflict of interest was prioritized, and the first move was to drop Roger Binny as selector of

the national team since his son Stuart Binny is a contender
for the national squad. Ravi Shastri's presence in the IPL
governing council was discontinued, and he has been
replaced by Sourav Ganguly. Anil Kumble, due to his role
as mentor of the Mumbai Indians and as a commentator,
was removed from the BCCI's technical committee,
while Ganguly was appointed its chairperson. Ganguly
has decided to no longer accept commentator positions,
so his conflict of interest no longer exists. As had been
rumoured, Srinivasan was replaced as the ICC chairman
by Manohar himself, six months ahead of the tenure's
completion. What was surprising however was that the
individual appointed to represent Manohar in case he was
unable to attend an ICC meeting, happened to be Sharad
Pawar rather than any other current board member.[7] The
nexus between politicians and cricket remains a concern,
one which is likely to crop up periodically within the IPL
and the BCCI going forward.

Later in November, perhaps due to the conflict of
interest issues, Kumble resigned from his role as mentor for
the Mumbai Indians. Sundar Raman, having resigned prior
to the board's AGM was appointed as the Reliance Group's
CEO for sports ventures shortly thereafter.[8] Assumedly, his
role would also include overseeing the Mumbai Indians,
so his connection with the IPL is likely to continue, albeit
now on the franchise side rather than the league side. The
fact that he has been unequivocally cleared by the Justice
Lodha Committee has also removed any ambiguity with
respect to his association with cricket.

The board won't have much time to make the changes,
but most of the intent has been positive. To really give

transparency a boost however, a respected outsider with impeccable credentials and administration experience, or a former player like Rahul Dravid whose acumen and reputation outweighs significant administrative experience, should eventually be given a chance to lead the IPL. The board has already suggested having three external members in the IPL governing council, in a departure from practices ever before. Eventually at the AGM, the suggestion was declined by the board, although there were some visible changes to the composition of the IPL governing council. This, however, was before the Justice Lodha Committee's specific recommendations, so it will be interesting to see which direction the modifications go.

It may not be an isolated realization, and it may well be the foresight to be proactive rather than reactive in order to preserve the autonomy of the board. It may also be the understanding that transparency and good governance are the only ways to both draw a clear distinction with Srinivasan's regime as well as create a lasting legacy of change. We'll know soon enough whether the board is proactive or the Justice Lodha Committee has been reactive. However, one way or the other, systemic change looks imminent. The period leading up to June will be the most testing period for the board as it hosts the ICC T20 World Cup and then segues into the riskiest season of the IPL yet. It's definitely not the easiest time to lead the embattled board unless one actually has plans to evolve and exorcise past failures. If it doesn't, martial law may be imposed upon it—either as a deterrent or as a lifestyle change.

There are also decisions that the BCCI itself needs to take in the next couple of months; decisions that the court will not take for it. The easy one is enforcing the directives, which is also a legacy-padding and defining one, to eradicate conflict of interest for officials, players and hangers-on. Policy is just one-tenth of the formula for success. Consistent tracking and enforcement is the key. This will effectively be the counter-Srinivasan move, and even on its own, its criticality cannot be overstated

What has not been easy to change or address is the way forward for the two suspended IPL franchises, and the overall treatment of the IPL. In principle, the decision is actually not that hard. For someone like Manohar or Thakur, terminating the franchises would be intuitive, but from the looks of it, the BCCI has become averse to litigation. Understandably so, since it hasn't really had a good day in the courts since Sreesanth and friends were taken into custody all the way back in 2013.

More than anything else, it will be the handling of the IPL and its franchises which will determine the IPL's legacy, and more importantly, its autonomy. If it takes a soft stand, no matter how much is done to bring the BCCI's matters into the public domain, it will mostly be forgotten. What a clumsily handled IPL decision could end up doing is to lead the court and its committees to intervene in other aspects. The court has not shown an inclination to terminate the franchises by its own order thus far, but in its observations it has implied that the BCCI could terminate the franchises. One interpretation for this is that the BCCI could terminate the franchises, and may receive the support of the court if the matter came before it on appeal by the terminated franchises.

Manohar and his team look the part of reformists and for now are best positioned to make the changes that bring the BCCI and the IPL into the real world of conformity. Yes, it's a wait-and-watch mode for the two-month period and beyond, but change will come to the board and to its trophy tournament, whether or not it is initiated by the new regime. Almost on cue, the board released a report on 31 October 2015 by the consulting firm KPMG. The report attributes the IPL's contribution to India's gross domestic product at INR1150 crore, and the IPL's total economic output to be INR2650 crore.[9] Through much of the BCCI–IPL's strife in recent years, the blame has been squarely placed on Srinivasan. Painting him as a villain and apportioning the entire blame on him for the governance lapse, the spot-fixing scandal and the conflict of interest controversy is perhaps unfair. From Srinivasan's perspective, he would be right to feel hard done by all of this. He has, of course, made some baffling decisions and tried to cling to the BCCI presidency in almost a surreal manner. That said, from his perspective, he has actually played with a reasonably straight bat. There is no question of shell ownership of the CSK at least until the recent transfer and/or sale of the team. The ill-fated Clause 6.2.4 may not have stood the judicial test, but it did at the time pave the way for him to have a dual role in Indian cricket. The Justice Mudgal Committee did absolve him of any active involvement with the scandal, barring his inaction in one instance. It was a combination of his autocratic manner of leading and his clumsy responses to obvious lapses that have led him to become the poster-child for all that is wrong with Indian cricket. It is a moniker that is a tad unfortunate, but when the dust settles, history might judge Srinivasan more kindly than the Indian public does today. If anything, his fault, at least from his point of view, was to be too open about his multiple roles and commercial interests in cricket! It's a conundrum, if any, given the full-throated support that transparency and accountability in cricket administration and the IPL are receiving.

This is, of course, assuming that the judiciary or any of its future committees doesn't come upon any damning inside information regarding the role of Srinivasan and India Cements in the current state of play within the BCCI and the IPL. Unless that happens, let's give him the benefit of doubt. He can be blamed for quite a lot, but clearly not for everything. One of the bigger external challenges for the IPL in the present day is that T20 cricket is already a diluted product that is saturating its viewing public. In just about nine years, 2007–16, there would already have been six ICC T2O World Cups held. This is in addition to not less than seven functional T20 leagues across the world, the IPL among them. The IPL's uniqueness is in that it is the only franchise league that features Indian players. But, despite the Indian players excelling in the IPL, the Indian team remains one of the middling performers on the international stage. Part of this is due to the rarity with which they play T20 internationals. Among the Test-playing nations, India has played the fewest T20 internationals, barring Bangladesh. There also doesn't seem to be a direct correlation between a successful domestic T20 league and a winning national team. Yes, three of the former winners have had reasonably good to very good domestic leagues—England, West Indies, and yes, India. But the two other South Asian countries that have won the T20 World Cup have little imprint on domestic franchise cricket—Pakistan and Sri Lanka. In fact, Sri Lanka is the most successful T20 cricket nation; yet most of their players didn't even get a place in the IPL rosters in 2015. For the BCCI, which needs to now show that its development programme from the grass roots and emphasis on the performance of the national team are paramount, the IPL is neither proving to be a farming system for unearthing exceptional Indian talent, nor is it helping to improve the quality of the Indian team's performance. If anything, the IPL has made stars of international players, and set into motion the freelance player movement, as I had mentioned in the introduction. So, if by providing exposure to Indian conditions, and money to sustain international players' careers, the Indian team would have underperformed in the T20 World Cup in India in March 2016, at least part of the blame would be apportioned to the IPL as a contributing factor. A commercial risk for the IPL in season nine is also that like in 2011, there could be saturation with cricket. And it could be a losing proposition any way it shapes up. If India outperforms expectations and wins the World Cup, it will be an emotional high that will be difficult to top, leading to disillusionment with the IPL. Conversely, if India underperforms at the World Cup, the anger and/ or disappointment with the performance could be taken out by the Indian fans on the IPL; they may even feel that an enthralling IPL season is a poor consolation prize after losing the World Cup title. In a season where so much will be there to prove, this added pressure won't be ideal for the BCCI–IPL.

The coming year or two will be extremely difficult for the IPL. On-field, it has to maintain consistency despite the off-field turbulence it is facing due to the conflict between the sponsorship requirements of eight teams, and the inability to rustle up eight able teams for the two upcoming seasons. The board will need to focus on its flagship property while at the same time work tirelessly to alter the public's perception, pre-empt the court and the Justice Lodha Committee, and modernize the way cricket is administered in today's day and age. For the IPL, the board must ensure that it remains scandal-free and retains control over the various elements that threaten to disrupt it. At the same time, it has to ensure that the product and sport are superior to the competition, and profitable for the franchise owners. The IPL suffered a reputation hit when the IPL governing council announced that it had ended the Champions League T20 due to lack of interest in it. Actually, this was a very good long-term move, and one which in the long run will help the IPL remain fresh and profitable. So at least from a fiscal and strategic point of view, this was a good move. The downside is that the successful franchises play even fewer matches in the current system than they would have earlier, and more importantly, the co-sanctioning boards of Australia and South Africa will need to be appeased somehow.

Off-field, the IPL will face a narrow path of most resistance within which it must operate. The conflict of interest controversy and the spot-fixing scandal have given reason to the court and to the Central government to regulate sports much more closely than ever before. Also of interest would be the once burning topic that has seemingly fallen off the radar but remains as important today as it was in 2013, and will likely be handed over to the Justice Lodha Committee to analyse and recommend in its third phase. This is the issue of the sealed envelope with names of stakeholders in cricket that the Justice Mudgal Committee submitted to the Supreme Court. It will be interesting to see what the punishment accorded to the offenders will be if their guilt is proven.[10] The legislations will perhaps be drafted and passed sooner rather than later if there is intent on the government's part. What this will mean is that a zero-tolerance policy will be in place, and the BCCI–IPL must tread a careful line. Again, the easiest way to do so would be to privatize the IPL, eliminate the auction, publicize the necessary information, and subject the franchise owners to rigorous disclosure and compliance requirements that would pass muster at any stage of scrutiny. To improve quality, it must create the structure of farming talent and commence a year-round training and competition system funded entirely by the 'cash-rich league'. The board can take the initiative to partner with the franchise owners and create world-class training and competition infrastructure that will eliminate the potential corruption caused by dependence on state associations, and give the franchises a chance to monetize their ownership through the year.

The IPL, despite Murphy's Law, has every opportunity to live up to its potential and create a Ricardian system of economic rent for everyone concerned.

Governance is going to be the most important word in the IPL's lexicon for the next five to seven years. As a term, governance is suitably vague, so let's look first at what the most comprehensive definition of good governance in sports is, as determined by the European Union's 'Expert Group on Good Governance' in 2013:[11]

> The framework and culture within which a sports body sets policy, delivers its strategic objectives, engages with stakeholders, monitors performance, evaluates and manages risk and reports to its constituents on its activities and progress including the delivery of effective, sustainable and proportionate sports policy and regulation.

To remain in compliance with good governance parameters and the principles of natural justice will be critical for the BCCI–IPL. So many of the components set out in this definition have no practical application within the IPL and the BCCI today. It will stand the board in good stead to familiarize itself with this terminology and use the good offices of its consultants to set this change in motion. The IPL governing council and the board, through the recommendations of its consultants, must be sure to implement and enforce them.

Merely seeking recommendations to help perception won't work for the board this time. Introducing a cricket ombudsman who can adjudicate disputes related to cricket will help in having checks and balances to the entire cricket set-up. It shouldn't be the court's prerogative to put forward a road map for effective and transparent governance for cricket and the IPL. As sport is a state subject under the Constitution of India, each state must adopt a uniform code of sports governance, development and ethics regulations, and implement them at a state level. However, given the limited success of such a measure, and given that even the court now has used the principle of public good, and indirectly, social benefit, we may now have a moral cause of action that grants the Central government a right to codify and pass legislation on sports as a national priority, to ensure that the citizens of India reap the pecuniary benefit of being a transparent and successful sporting nation. The BCCI–IPL must do all it can to prevent that from coming to be. Otherwise, its entire autonomy is going to be lost as the court is quite likely to focus on an external audit to gauge the prevalence of unethical activity, while staffing a preliminary task force to liaise with the states and the Centre towards formulating legislation that has bicameral enforceability. It will allow the BCCI the due process it deserves, and let the committees issue directives as they see fit. It's the way to ensure that the greater public good will be served.

The IPL should by now have used the first-mover advantage to its optimal end. It didn't because of various setbacks, scandals, complacency and an evolving degree of judicial involvement which eventually point towards greater governance and transparent integrity.

The IPL however has done many great things for Indian culture, society and sports. As the first-in-time professional sports league or event, it has created a blueprint that helps commercialize sports in India, and has been successfully emulated by various different sports in India. The IPL created magic out of dust, building a powerhouse entity comparable to the world's best sports leagues in a matter of years, rather than decades. The IPL imprinted itself upon Indian society, and by blending entertainment with glamour and sport, it created the perfect initial formula for success. By bringing corporates into ownership positions and creating a sports culture around a next-generation format of the game, it truly took cricket into the twenty-first century, and made India the centre of the T20 universe. I had mentioned earlier that many of the initial goals and the original intent was one which created an ecosystem for a scalable sports league, one which would evolve both for itself as well as for those invested in it. So the four-billion-dollar question is whether the IPL can turn it around and become all that it aspired to be. Manohar's return means an external perception that conflict of interest will be addressed and corrected. It also means that some of the younger members of the BCCI will be allowed to work towards improving processes in line with global best practices. Many times in the recent past, one has got the feeling that the court is waiting for the BCCI–IPL to just show intent to improve. Now is the time to do it. Put independent former players in positions of decision-making and let them create an environment where learning and growth is fostered, and future lapses in integrity avoided. Create a players' grievance association or board to provide them guidance and representation when needed. Professionalize the player–agent accreditation process and ensure that no effort is spared to render the IPL corruption-free. It may be too late to avoid judicial intervention every time the BCCI–IPL falters, but that is no one's fault but the BCCI's own. It will need to accept it as a regrettable necessity and move forward with its own objective and proactive improvements. Eventually, if the IPL shows integrity and intent, and has put in place processes that can't easily be breached, has avoided conflicts of interest, and is not overrun by the BCCI or those associated with it, it may get the independence to operate. If there is one thing we have learnt, it's that the judiciary has, at least until now, been unwilling to interfere until compelled to. As long as the interests of the most important stakeholder—the Indian cricket fan—are being respected and looked after, the principles of natural justice are being served.

Will the IPL always be at the centre of controversy? Well, being a leader and a snazzy, jazzy, million-watt, high-octane target means the IPL will always be susceptible to scandal. The large amounts of money involved and the power players who make the IPL tick will mean that the league will always be high-risk and will have its detractors. If it does things right this time around, it could minimize and mitigate those factors and detractors. The IPL hasn't adequately sold the sport and hasn't provided the requisite respect to the Indian fan in its previous avatar. If it can reverse both aspects, watch out. It seems there are other plans afoot for T20 cricket in India—perhaps realizing that the optimal size of the IPL, given the limitation of time in the calendar, is eight teams, not six, not ten, not twelve, *just eight.* So, what does that mean when it comes to expansion, globalization, world domination and achieving critical mass? No one really knows. It does appear however that the IPL will be left to do its own thing as an autarky that requires no outside influence, replete with controversy, cricket, and cash. But the BCCI, recognizing the opportunity for a larger presence in the world of

T20 league cricket, apparently appears to be considering floating another domestic T20 league that is independent of the IPL. In an interview with a leading business daily, Anurag Thakur put the thought out there, but did not elucidate how it would play out if the BCCI had two competing leagues in place. He also did not elaborate on where the space in the international calendar would come from, if even the IPL was unable to command a wider window for an expanded schedule.[12] It is nonetheless an interesting concept, although until the IPL cleans up its act in entirety, a second in-house league will be fraught with problems from the get-go.

Think of it this way. In its first nine years, the IPL irked the media, strong-armed its sponsors, terminated and at times harassed its franchises, got caught in a massive conflict of interest scandal, and fans were cheated when matches were allegedly fixed. It got sued repeatedly losing most of its battles, and the BCCI had and continues to have its dirty laundry washed embarrassingly in front of the public. The Champions League T20 has been abandoned because it was so uninspiring that its relevance no longer existed in a cricket-crazy country. It has done most things wrong if one looks at it objectively, but it is still so relevant to Indian society. It is still the leading sports league in India. It is still the leading T20 cricket league in the world. If the IPL is still generating massive viewership and hasn't seen a significant dip in sponsorship revenue yet, no one can possibly rule out its freak potential if it actually gets things in order. It will be harder to turn things around, and there are now internal and external threats. There is also the uncertainty of the unknown.

There will be strife before there is relief, and for the next
year or so at least, the board and the IPL will be on somewhat
uncertain footing, dabbling frequently with litigation,
and trying to make sense of how the recommendations
can be implemented uniformly. The board faces many
challenges internally and externally. Since the Justice
Lodha Committee's recommendations being submitted
to the Supreme Court, the board has been in constant
dialogue with those most affected—the state associations
and those hampered by conflict of interest restrictions.
And in an ironic twist of fate, the behemoth that the BCCI
has become—with over thirty full-member associations
having voting rights, and many more associate, affiliate
and future members—could be its Achilles heel. Getting
a consensus of any sort is going to be an onerous task,
and the BCCI stands to be a victim of the behemoth it has
created itself. The odds are, of course, stacked against the
board in 2016.[13] Here's where it stands. In early February
2016, just a month after the committee had submitted its
recommendation, the Supreme Court directed the board to
comply with the recommendations within a month, i.e. by
3 March 2016. The board has since faced struggles within,
and many of the member associations have rejected some
or most of the committee's recommendations outright. The
board assembled a special general meeting on 19 February
2016 to discuss the committee's recommendations, where
it was decided that the board would file an affidavit
with the Supreme Court seeking clarifications on the
'anomalies and difficulties' regarding the Justice Lodha
Committee recommendations. Also discussed at the time
and since acted upon were independent pleas by multiple

state associations seeking clarifications and relief from the judiciary for the adverse impact that the committee's recommendations would have on them. This was a measure recommended by the board so as to lend weight to opposing the recommendations. The board and the IPL are in an unenviable position today, with an extremely short time frame given to them in which to incorporate radical changes across the cricket administration. With the Supreme Court seemingly unwilling to be flexible and appearing to be running out of patience on any delaying tactics, it is a very tall order for the board to be compliant and, additionally, to get its state associations on board as well.[14] On 1 March 2016, the board submitted an exhaustive affidavit to the Supreme Court, stating its differences with some of the Justice Lodha Committee's recommendations. In particular, the differences mentioned in the nearly sixty-page document included the following: the recommendation wherein each state had only one vote; the potentially problematic reduction of advertisement time and opportunities for broadcast of matches; the inclusion of the CAG's nominee in the committee and the council— the board deeming it unconstitutional and in violation of its constitution that exclude non-members from being part of the managing committee, while also declaring it as a violation of the ICC's rules and a possible cause for the BCCI's derecognition from the ICC; similarly, the board opposed having representatives of two franchises in the IPL governing council; the barrier on reappointment for members of the managing committee as well as the cooling-off period; the restriction on politicians; the curb on the holding of dual posts, i.e. in a state association and the

BCCI simultaneously; the maximum age ceiling of seventy years for office-bearers; the concept of a board-funded players' association; dispensing with some of the BCCI committees; bringing the BCCI under the RTI; and lastly, legalizing betting.[15]

The concerns were heard by the Supreme Court on 3 March 2016 and the court's initial reaction wasn't indulgent. There does, however, seem to be the possibility that some of the recommendations by the Justice Lodha Committee may be reviewed or assessed over time, although that is far from certain. What is certain however is that discussions, disputes and uncertainty regarding the IPL and the BCCI with respect to compliance with directives, and the future of Indian cricket, will likely continue for an extended period ahead. It promises to be riveting, and what could add to the intrigue are two further developments recently. Towards the end of February 2016 came the news of a potential shake-up in the Bengaluru franchise over the next couple of years. Pursuant to the off-field uncertainty that the RCB's owner, Vijay Mallya, has faced in the last few years, going forward, he is expected to have a role in the franchise that is equivalent to that of a Chief Mentor, where the management of the affiliate that will run the RCB may consult him if they choose to.[16] Also rumoured to be part of the deal is the presence of his son, Siddharth Mallya, for a period of two years on the board of the affiliate that will run the team. While this could mean that the future of the team is secure for the next few years at least, that isn't a foregone conclusion by any means. And to cap it all off, the ED received approval from a special court to begin proceedings to extradite Lalit

Modi to India in order to face charges related to alleged violations.[17] Is this the end of Modi's influence directly or indirectly on cricket? We'll find out soon enough as he may make his awaited return to Indian shores, although not on his own terms.

All in all, things are hurtling towards an impasse, and as we head into IPL IX, one gets the feeling that this coming year will be one of the most eventful off-pitch seasons in the history of Indian cricket. By the time IPL X comes around, no one knows what complexion all of this may take. And let's not forget the already existing challenges.

Competition is going to be one of the main threats. Internal competition with other sports leagues will over time be a challenge, although not immediately. External competition with other T20 leagues contracting players and possibly diluting the product offering of the IPL is another threat. Revenues drying up in the absence of new verticals will lead to increasing costs and lower returns, taking also into account the changing dynamics between franchises and the central IPL. Reputation and perception will continue to be upward challenges to overcome, and the next couple of editions will be critical, especially depending on how the BCCI–IPL tackles the eight-franchise threshold. The Supreme Court has already accepted the Justice Lodha Committee's recommendations and reprimanded the board and the IPL severely. A very real risk if things don't improve is that the entire IPL may just be suspended indefinitely by the court. It has certainly indicated its zero-tolerance policy going forward. The new world order in cricket could shake the very fundamentals of world cricket and render the ICC and the BCCI redundant bodies. The exposés that we the public are frequently treated to could also lead to some unforgivable truths and lead to the demise of the IPL as we know it. The biggest threat to the IPL however is the IPL itself and the board that controls it. Fix that, make it independent, and professionalize it; and the IPL has a fighting chance to recover. In 2017, the broadcast rights for the IPL will be up for grabs, and by all indications it ought to be record-setting in the Indian context. The IPL even today is a coveted property for broadcasters because of the various key demographics it targets. So, much like the EPL did in 2015, the IPL too is likely to bolster its value from 2017 onwards. It need not snatch defeat from the jaws of victory, and if it really means to change, the board should by then have privatized the IPL and made it a professionally run league that competes with the world's best, and gives Indian fans the holistic and complete viewing and league experience.

Not out in its first eight innings in consistently worsening conditions, the incredible IPL must now adopt a more inclusive and environment-friendly strategy if it's to maintain its unbeaten streak in the distant future. Till now, we have seen the fad component and the fizzle component. The next few years will tell us if the first-in-time IPL turns it around and builds upon a golden opportunity. The IPL has never believed in half measures—now would not be a good time to reverse that trend.

Notes

Chapter 1

1. 17 November 2015. 'Banned IPL Players Had Dawood Link, Says Ex-top Cop Despite Clean Chit'. NDTV.
    http://www.ndtv.com/video/player/the-buck-stops-here/banned-ipl-players-had-dawood-link-says-ex-top-cop-despite-clean-chit/391117
    Also refer to Kumar, Neeraj, *Dial D for Don: Inside Stories of CBI Case Missions*. New Delhi: Penguin, 2015, pp 252–53.
2. Suresh, Appu Esthose. 27 August 2015. 'Family emails say Lalit Modi owns "interest" in 3 IPL teams, lawyer says that's "guesswork"'. *Indian Express*.
    http://indianexpress.com/article/india/india-others/family-emails-say-lalit-modi-owns-interest-in-3-ipl-teams-lawyer-says-thats-guesswork/
3. 18 September 2015. 'Preity Zinta-Lalit Modi email: "Keep this to yourself, no one should know about it"'. Zee Media Bureau.
    http://zeenews.india.com/sports/cricket/preity-zinta-lalit-modi-email-keep-this-to-yourself-no-one-should-know-about-it_1798942.html
4. Mahajan, Rohit, and Mukherjee, Arindam. 3 May 2010. 'Captain Crony Capital'. *Outlook*.
    http://www.outlookindia.com/article/captain-crony-capital/265185

5.   Assisi, Charles, Raghunath, Abhishek, and Bharadwaj, Vijay.
     25 May 2010. 'The Rise and Fall of Lalit Modi'. *Forbes.*
     http://www.forbes.com/2010/05/25/forbes-india-rise-and-
     fall-lalit-modi.html
6.   Sundaresan, Bharat. 19 June 2015. 'BCCI's Arun Jaitley panel
     had indicted Lalit Modi for favouring Adani'. *Indian Express.*
     http://indianexpress.com/article/sports/cricket/bccis-arun-
     jaitley-panel-had-indicted-lalit-modi-for-favouring-adani/
7.   25 June 2015. 'Lalit Modi says he signed Kochi bid in IPL
     under pressure'. ABP Live.
     http://www.abplive.in/india-news/lalit-modi-says-he-
     signed-kochi-bid-in-ipl-under-pressure-23157
8.   23 April 2010. 'IPL: Details Tharoor sought were not
     classified'. NDTV.
     http://www.ndtv.com/india-news/ipl-details-tharoor-
     sought-were-not-classified-416173
9.   Chacko, Saji. 28 September 2013. 'Lalit downfall started
     with tweet on Kochi franchise'. *Sunday Guardian.*
     http://www.sunday-guardian.com/investigation/lalit-
     downfall-started-with-tweet-on-kochi-franchise
10. Mathew, Liz, and Mehra Dayal, Priyanka. 13 April 2010.
     'IPL spat turns nastier, gets political hue'. *Mint.*
     http://www.livemint.com/Home-Page/
     xxvzKOmZJclZwW5yDjcNbM/IPL-spat-turns-nastier-
     gets-political-hue.html
11. Sundaresan, Bharat. 15 June 2015. 'Lalit Modi's fall
     from grace, his powerful backers and continuing battle
     with rivals'. *Indian Express.*
     http://indianexpress.com/article/sports/cricket/the-world-
     of-lalit-controversy-modi/
12. Chacko, Saji. 28 September 2013. 'Lalit downfall started with
     tweet on kochi franchise'. *Sunday Guardian.*
     http://www.sunday-guardian.com/investigation/lalit-
     downfall-started-with-tweet-on-kochi-franchise
13. Mahajan, Rohit, and Mukherjee, Arindam. 3 May 2010.
     'Captain Crony Capital'. *Outlook.*
     http://www.outlookindia.com/article/captain-crony-
     capital/265185

14. Bose, Soumitra. 4 June 2013. 'Gurunath Meiyappan: A king-size Chennai super doosra'. NDTV. http://www.ndtv.com/people/gurunath-meiyappan-a-king-size-chennai-super-doosra-523235

15. 15 May 2012. 'IPL 2012: BCCI suspends five players accused in spot-fixing'. Cricket Country. http://www.cricketcountry.com/news/ipl-2012-bcci-suspends-five-players-accused-in-spot-fixing-14619

16. Dorries, Ben. 10 August 2015. 'Indian Premier League founder Lalit Modi reveals plans for new world cricket governing body'. *Daily Telegraph.* http://www.dailytelegraph.com.au/sport/cricket/indian-premier-league-founder-lalit-modi-reveals-plans-for-new-world-cricket-governing-body/story-fni2fnmo-1227477000963

17. Ugra, Sharda. 17 January 2014. 'Big Three could control revamped ICC'. ESPN Cricinfo. http://www.espncricinfo.com/ci-icc/content/story/710723.html

18. 19 April 2013. 'No end to Indian Cricket League dispute'. Cricbuzz. http://www.cricbuzz.com/cricket-news/10879/no-end-to-indian-cricket-league-dispute

19. 19 October 2015. 'Chris Cairns told players to assist match-fixing or "never play again"'. *Guardian.* http://www.theguardian.com/sport/2015/oct/19/chris-cairns-match-fixing-threat-never-play-again

20. Interview of Lalit Modi conducted by Mihir Bose. Lalitmodi.com. http://www.lalitmodi.com/pages.php?id=6

21. Assisi, Charles, Raghunath, Abhishek, and Bharadwaj, Vijay. 25 May 2010. 'The Rise and Fall of Lalit Modi'. *Forbes.* http://www.forbes.com/2010/05/25/forbes-india-rise-and-fall-lalit-modi.html

22. 18 December 2007. 'IPL lays out revenue-sharing plan with franchises'. ESPN Cricinfo. http://www.espncricinfo.com/ipl/content/story/326200.html

24 January 2008. 'Big business and Bollywood grab stakes in IPL'. ESPN Cricinfo.
http://www.espncricinfo.com/ipl/content/story/333193.html

23.   Malik, Ashok. 30 March 2010. 'Pass the gravy'. ESPN Cricinfo.
http://www.espncricinfo.com/magazine/content/story/453945.html

24.   Engineer, Tariq, and Gollapudi, Nagraj. 30 June 2010. 'BCCI cancels IPL rights deal with WSG'. ESPN Cricinfo.
http://www.espncricinfo.com/india/content/story/465322.html

25.   Engineer, Tariq. 11 August 2010. 'MSM petition over facilitation fee arbitration dismissed'. 11 August 2010. ESPN Cricinfo.
http://www.espncricinfo.com/indian-premier-league-2011/content/story/471991.html

26.   24 January 2014. 'SC allows arbitration between WSG, MSM on IPL broadcast rights'. Press Trust of India.
http://timesofindia.indiatimes.com/news/SC-allows-arbitration-between-WSG-MSM-on-IPL-broadcast-rights/articleshow/29314005.cms

27.   Binoy, George. 26 April 2010. 'The "facilitation fee" furore'. ESPN Cricinfo.
http://www.espncricinfo.com/ipl2010/content/story/457318.html

28.   Guha, Ramachandra. 1 June 2013. 'The serpent in the garden'. ESPN Cricinfo.
http://www.espncricinfo.com/magazine/content/story/638602.html

29.   Ugra, Sharda. 28 May 2012. 'The IPL earns its cricket cred'. ESPN Cricinfo.
http://www.espncricinfo.com/indian-premier-league-2012/content/story/566524.html

Chapter 2

1. 14 July 2015. 'Indian Premier League Spot-Fixing: The Timeline'. Cricketnext.
    http://www.ibnlive.com/cricketnext/news/indian-premier-league-spot-fixing-the-timeline-1044845.html
2. 14 July 2015. 'IPL 2013 spot-fixing controversy: Timeline'. *Business Standard.*
    http://www.business-standard.com/article/news-ians/ipl-2013-spot-fixing-controversy-timeline-115071400947_1.html
3. 21 September 2013. 'IPL: Asad Rauf charged in IPL spot-fixing scandal'. BBC.
    http://www.bbc.com/sport/cricket/24187476
4. Karhadkar, Amol. 20 February 2015. 'Kundra set for Rajasthan Royals exit'. ESPN Cricinfo.
    http://www.espncricinfo.com/india/content/story/835499.html
5. 14 July 2015. 'India Cements shares plunge 6% as SC panel suspends CSK from IPL for 2 years'. Firstpost.
    http://www.firstpost.com/sports/india-cements-shares-plunge-6-sc-panel-suspends-csk-ipl-2-years-2341598.html
6. Menon, Vishal. 27 July 2015. 'S Sreesanth begs for a chance'. *Indian Express.*
    http://indianexpress.com/article/sports/cricket/teary-eyed-sree-begs-for-a-chance/

Chapter 3

1. Engineer, Tariq. 11 October 2010. 'Lawyers question IPL teams' expulsion'. NDTV.
    http://sports.ndtv.com/cricket/news/156279-lawyers-question-ipl-teams-expulsion
2. Aprameya, C. 25 October 2012. 'Half price sale: IPL team purchased'. thatscricket.com
    http://www.thatscricket.com/news/2012/10/25/half-price-sale-ipl-team-purchased-064899.html

3.   Babu, Gireesh, and Narasimhan, T.E. 15 June 2015. '2G scam casts big shadow on Maran's Sun Network'. *Business Standard*. http://www.business-standard.com/article/companies/2g-scam-casts-big-shadow-on-maran-s-sun-network-115061501110_1.html

4.   Pandey, Devendra. 19 August 2015. 'Preity Zinta to IPL officials: Some of my players may have been linked to suspicious activity'. *Indian Express*. http://indianexpress.com/article/sports/cricket/some-of-my-players-may-have-been-linked-to-suspicious-activity-preity-zinta-to-ipl-officials/
     19 August 2015. 'Claims of Kings XI players throwing games false: Preity Zinta'. *Hindustan Times*. http://www.hindustantimes.com/cricket/claims-of-kings-xi-players-throwing-games-false-preity-zinta/story-89lxQYIPkKYsweZ1FHkOSI.html

5.   27 October 2010. 'Kochi gets termination notice'. ESPN Cricinfo. http://www.espncricinfo.com/indian-premier-league-2011/content/current/story/483762.html

6.   8 July 2015. 'Arbitrator asks BCCI to pay 550 crore to Kochi Tuskers!'. Press Trust of India. http://www.rediff.com/cricket/report/arbitrator-asks-bcci-to-pay-550-crore-to-kochi-tuskers-ipl-india-cricket/20150708.htm

7.   Laha, Somshuvra. 2 April 2013. 'Not granted window but IPL still thrives'. *Hindustan Times*. http://www.hindustantimes.com/india/not-granted-window-but-ipl-still-thrives/story-s9pgXCXlVHjnkwxLw86XaI.html

8.   23 April 2015. 'Chennai Super Kings valued at just Rs 5 lakh only by owners'. *India Today*. http://indiatoday.intoday.in/story/chennai-super-kings-valuation-rs-5-lakh-by-owners/1/431665.html

9.   April 2015. 'On a sticky wicket: A concise report on brand values in the Indian Premier League'. American Appraisal India Private Limited.

http://american-appraisal.in/AA-Files/Images_IN/PDF/BrandValuesIPL_April2015.pdf

10. 'History of the English Premier League'. SuperSport. http://www.supersport.com/football/english-premier-league/content.aspx?id=20420

11. 2014. Excerpt taken from the Justice Mudgal IPL Probe Committee report, vol. 1, p 43.

12. NDTV. http://sports.ndtv.com/cricket/videos/ipl-scam-chennai-super-kings-could-face-termination-observes-supreme-court-346359

13. 16 July 2015. 'BCCI can terminate franchises—Lodha'. http://www.espncricinfo.com/india/content/story/899293.html

14. 8 December 2015. 'Reverse bidding, tenders and two new teams: BCCI set to take decision over new-look IPL'. Firstpost. http://www.firstpost.com/sports/star-india-chettinad-cement-among-21-companies-to-buy-ipl-bid-document-for-two-new-teams-2535964.html?utm_medium=twitter&utm_source=twitterfeed

15. Ananth, Venkat, and Choudhary, Vidhi. 9 December 2015. 'Pune, Rajkot new teams for 2016 Indian Premier League'. *Mint.* http://www.livemint.com/Consumer/4bxgtBgHrgCqkk7uDeh5JP/New-IPL-teams-Sanjeev-Goenka-wins-Pune-Intex-Group-gets-Ra.html

16. 8 December 2015. 'Pune, Rajkot to host new IPL franchises'. ESPN Cricinfo. http://www.espncricinfo.com/India/content/story/949987.html

17. Sundaresan, Bharat. 19 July 2015. 'BCCI's Arun Jaitley panel had indicted Lalit Modi for favouring Adani'. *Indian Express.* http://indianexpress.com/article/sports/cricket/bccis-arun-jaitley-panel-had-indicted-lalit-modi-for-favouring-adani/

18. 15 April 2010. 'Who own IPL teams?' *Deccan Herald.* http://www.deccanherald.com/content/63959/who-own-ipl-teams.html

Chapter 4

1.   Sundaresan, Bharat. 18 February 2016. 'Harbhajan Singh, others land in conflict zone'.
      http://indianexpress.com/article/sports/cricket/harbhajan-singh-bhajji-bcci-sourav-ganguly-conflict-of-interest-anurag-thakur-india/#sthash.GprMfew7.dpuf

2.   15 December 2014. 'Supreme Court to hear BCCI clause amendments'. ESPN Cricinfo.
      http://www.espncricinfo.com/india/content/story/810499.html

3.   17 December 2014. 'Sunil Gavaskar, Ravi Shastri, Sourav Ganguly in BCCI's list of people with conflict of interest'. Cricbuzz.
      http://serpens.cricbuzz.com/cricket-news/67465/sunil-gavaskar-ravi-shastri-sourav-ganguly-in-bccis-list-of-people-with-conflict-of-interest

4.   Choudhary, Vidhi. 17 November 2015. 'Reliance hires Sundar Raman to head sports unit'.
      http://www.livemint.com/Companies/nMNIJMkqnvH1S4jpvxm8ZL/Reliance-hires-Sundar-Raman-to-head-sports-unit.html

5.   23 April 2010. 'Poorna Patel leaked no e-mail: IPL'. *The Hindu*.
      http://www.thehindu.com/news/national/poorna-patel-leaked-no-email-ipl/article408643.ece

6.   22 April 2010. 'Praful Patel's PS sent new franchisee valuations to Tharoor'. *Times of India*.
      http://timesofindia.indiatimes.com/India/Praful-Patels-PS-sent-new-franchisee-valuations-to-Tharoor/articleshow/5843395.cms

7.   Phukan, Sandeep, and Doshi, Anjali. 22 April 2010. 'Multiple allegations about Praful email to Tharoor'. NDTV.
      http://www.ndtv.com/india-news/multiple-allegations-about-praful-email-to-tharoor-416090

8.   Ibid.

9.   V., Manju. 23 April 2010. 'Praful Patel's daughter pulled out scheduled AI flight for IPL'. *Times of India.* http://timesofindia.indiatimes.com/india/Praful-Patels-daughter-pulled-out-scheduled-AI-flight-for-IPL/articleshow/5846394.cms

10.   Sundaresan, Bharat. 15 June 2015. 'Lalit Modi's fall from grace, his powerful backers and continuing battle with rivals'. *Indian Express.* http://indianexpress.com/article/sports/cricket/the-world-of-lalit-controversy-modi/

11.   17 December 2014. 'Sunil Gavaskar, Ravi Shastri, Sourav Ganguly in BCCI's list of people with conflict of interest'. Cricbuzz. http://serpens.cricbuzz.com/cricket-news/67465/sunil-gavaskar-ravi-shastri-sourav-ganguly-in-bccis-list-of-people-with-conflict-of-interest

12.   14 July 2015. 'IPL scandal: Chennai Super Kings and Rajasthan Royals suspended'. BBC. http://www.bbc.com/news/world-asia-india-33517583

13.   Venugopal, Arun. 29 September 2015. 'Supreme Court rejects BCCI conflict-of-interest plea'. ESPN Cricinfo. http://www.espncricinfo.com/india/content/story/924465.html

14.   Basra, Sukhwant. 22 July 2015. 'Ridden by conflict of interest, BCCI lets fans down again'. *Hindustan Times.* http://www.hindustantimes.com/cricket/ridden-by-conflict-of-interest-bcci-lets-fans-down-again/story-Kq2kmcHIWf40aXOyvXzWVI.html

15.   Kesavan, Mukul. 28 March 2014. 'Indian cricket's conflict-of-interest problem'. ESPN Cricinfo. http://www.espncricinfo.com/magazine/content/story/731687.html

16.   Rautray, Samanwaya. 18 December 2014. 'Court questions conflict of interest in cricket fiefdom'. *Economic Times.* http://articles.economictimes.indiatimes.com/2014-12-18/news/57196595_1_n-srinivasan-ipl-teams-indian-premier-league

17.   5 December 2015. 'BCCI has too many politicians: Ian Chappell. Press Trust of India.
       http://www.livemint.com/Politics/
       KTOZsUKjWCXT9MbwsuwoGO/BCCI-has-too-many-
       politicians-Ian-Chappell.html

Chapter 5

1.   Mahajan, Rohit, and Mukherjee, Arindam. 3 May 2010. 'Captain Crony Capital'.
      http://www.outlookindia.com/article/captain-crony-
      capital/265185
      17 June 2015. 'Sushma Swaraj, Vasundhara Raje helped me: Lalit Modi'. *The Hindu.*
      http://www.thehindu.com/news/national/sushma-
      swaraj-vasundhara-raje-helped-me-lalit-modi/
      article7323174.ece

Chapter 6

1.   Rao, K. Shriniwas. 28 January 2011. 'Was IPL auction fair? Mumbai Indians raise questions'. *Times of India.*
      http://timesofindia.indiatimes.com/news/was-IPL-
      auction-fair-Mumbai-Indians-raise-questions/
      articleshow/7375330.cms?
2.   10 February 2015. 'Premier League in record £5.14bn TV rights deal'. BBC.
      http://www.bbc.com/news/business-31379128
3.   Brown, Maury. 10 December 2014. 'Major League Baseball Sees Record $9 Billion In Revenues For 2014'. *Forbes.*
      http://www.forbes.com/sites/maurybrown/2014/12/10/
      major-league-baseball-sees-record-9-billion-in-revenues-
      for-2014/
4.   Newman, Maria. 18 March 2005. 'Congress Opens Hearings on Steroid Use in Baseball'. *New York Times.*
      http://www.nytimes.com/learning/teachers/featured_
      articles/20050318friday.html

5. Badenhausen, Kurt. 15 July 2015. 'The World's 50 Most Valuable Sports Teams 2015'. *Forbes*.
    http://www.forbes.com/sites/kurtbadenhausen/2015/07/15/the-worlds-50-most-valuable-sports-teams-2015/

6. 9 July 2015. 'ISL 2015 Player Auction and Draft Rules'.
    http://www.indiansuperleague.com/news/2114-isl-player-auction-and-draft-rules

Chapter 7

1. 5 June 2015. 'Pepsi IPL 2015 viewership 21% higher than previous year'. *Business Standard*.
    http://www.business-standard.com/article/current-affairs/pepsi-ipl-2015-viewership-21-higher-than-previous-year-115060401095_1.html

2. Mohanarangan, Vinayakk. 27 October 2015. 'IPL is still a big brand, says BCCI secretary Anurag Thakur'. Firstpost.
    http://www.firstpost.com/sports/ipl-is-still-a-big-brand-says-bcci-secretary-anurag-thakur-2483480.html?utm_medium=twitter&utm_source=twitterfeed

3. Farooq, Umar. 5 December 2015. 'Everything you need to know about the PSL'. ESPN Cricinfo.
    http://www.espncricinfo.com/pakistan/content/story/948897.html

4. 8 December 2015. 'Pune, Rajkot to host new IPL franchises'. ESPN Cricinfo.
    http://www.espncricinfo.com/india/content/story/949987.html

5. Chakraborty, Amlan. 26 November 2015. 'ICC chief Shashank Manohar pans "bullying" by "Big Three"'. *Mint*.
    http://www.livemint.com/Politics/dRS4pCo6s53hAK2QB5Ey5O/ICC-chief-Shashank-Manohar-pans-bullying-by-Big-Three.html

6. Ananth, Venkat. 16 October 2015. 'BCCI engages Deloitte to undertake Project Transformation'. *Mint*.
    http://www.livemint.com/Consumer/P43ZyuYK2AQPIt6xNPMQwO/BCCI-engages-Deloitte-to-undertake-Project-Transformation.html

7.   Vishwanathan, Siddharth. 9 November 2015. 'Board of Control for Cricket in India AGM: Ravi Shastri out of IPL Panel, Sourav Ganguly is in, 10 Developments'. NDTV. http://sports.ndtv.com/cricket/news/251497-board-of-control-for-cricket-in-india-agm-ravi-shastri-out-of-ipl-panel-sourav-ganguly-is-in-10-developments

8.   3 November 2015. 'Sundar Raman resigns as IPL COO, BCCI accepts resignation'. *Times of India*. http://timesofindia.indiatimes.com/sports/ipl/news/Sundar-Raman-resigns-as-IPL-COO-BCCI-accepts-resignation/articleshow/49640886.cms

9.   31 October 2015. 'IPL economics'. *Mint*. http://www.livemint.com/Opinion/xn4kZ3ufsjkP3zQ23XQlGN/IPL-economics.html

10.   Engineer, Tariq. 9 February 2016. 'Forget Sunil Dev's allegations against Dhoni: What did BCCI do with Mudgal Committee's sealed envelope?'. Firstpost. http://www.firstpost.com/sports/forget-sunil-devs-allegations-against-dhoni-what-did-bcci-do-with-mudgal-committees-sealed-envelope-2617236.html

11.   September 2013. EU Work Plan for Sport. http://ec.europa.eu/sport/library/policy_documents/xg-gg-201307-dlvrbl2-sept2013.pdf

12.   Choudhary, Vidhi. 10 December 2015. 'BCCI could look at the option of one more T20 league: Anurag Thakur'. http://www.livemint.com/Consumer/Yh0u0CFkSRThL7jHJTE2mI/BCCI-could-look-at-the-option-of-one-more-T20-league.html

13.   Engineer, Tariq. 5 February 2016. 'The BCCI has to change but we must be cautious in implementing the Lodha Committee report'. Firstpost. http://www.firstpost.com/sports/the-bcci-has-to-change-but-we-must-be-cautious-in-implementing-the-lodha-committee-report-2613394.html

14. Venugopal, Arun. 22 February 2016. 'MCA to file intervention application on Lodha report'. ESPN Cricinfo. http://www.espncricinfo.com/india/content/story/975317.html

15. Gollapudi, Nagraj. 3 March 2016. 'Supreme Court takes exception to BCCI's views on Lodha report'. ESPN Cricinfo. http://www.espncricinfo.com/india/content/story/978109.html

16. Fraser, Douglas. 28 February 2016. 'The King of Good Times, de-throned'. BBC. http://www.bbc.com/news/uk-scotland-scotland-business-35681740?ocid=fbindia

17. Narayan, Khushboo. 2 March 2016. 'Case against Lalit Modi: ED gets court nod to begin extradition'. *Indian Express*. http://indianexpress.com/article/india/india-news-india/case-against-lalit-modi-ed-gets-court-nod-to-begin-extradition/#sthash.7zISVBnH.dpuf